SLOW DOWN!
Children are Learning!

Effective strategies to support overall achievement by focusing on developmental growth in elementary classrooms

Erin Mengeu

DOWNLOAD YOUR FREE TEACHING RESOURCES

FREE RESOURCE PACKETS

Just to say thanks for buying my book,
I have provided some of the resources mentioned
as free downloadable resource packets from my web site.

A square thumbnail like the one above appears
each time a free resource is mentioned in the book.

**To download your free resource packets go to:
betheirdifference.com/slow-down-
teacher-resource-packet/**

Want/Need Credit Hours?

Learn with Me

Get credit hours for the hard work you already put into your classroom. Visit the link below to see how.

www.betheirdifference.com/online-graduate-courses-for-teacher-professional-development/

This book was written for every teacher who wants to make a life impact on the students they teach.

Contents

INTRODUCTION

Developmental Growth is the Key to a Student's Overall Achievement.

I couldn't believe what my friend was telling me—I just couldn't understand. A former student of mine had considered ending his life. That's right, my former student considered hurting himself. This could not be right, especially this student! But it was.

As an elementary teacher, I've always enjoyed keeping up with how my former students are doing. I love seeing them blossom into who they were meant to be. I love hearing about their graduation and what they are moving onto in life. But this time was different. This was the first time that the news I was hearing about a former student was devastating.

If you are reading this book, then I know you can relate. We teachers build relationships with our students, and we love them like they are our own! At least I do. But I'm pretty sure you do too! We care about each child who walks into our room.

Let me just say that this phone call got my wheels turning. I couldn't stop thinking about it. Thank God his parents got to him in time. I didn't know the whole story at first, only what I was hearing from my friend on the phone. All she knew at the time was that he was meeting with a campus counselor and the counselor contacted his parents and asked them to come and get him immediately. Whatever the circumstances were, I was glad that he was getting help and thankful for the counselor who had alerted his parents.

As I processed the information that was shared with me, I started to think about the kind of kid Brian was when he was in my 3rd grade class. He was smart. He was fun. He had lots of friends. He made good choices. He really seemed to have it all together—at least on the outside. One would assume that he would progress through his school years and become whatever he set his mind on becoming. In middle school, Brian was on the Academic Challenge Team and had a good group of friends. In high school he was in the band and into computer science.

You see, this was not a troubled child coming from a troubled family. He wasn't making bad choices in his life. He wasn't a kid with a chip on his shoulder. He was a kid who seemed to have it all together.

As the wheels were turning in my head, I had so many questions: Where did it go wrong? Could this have been prevented? Did he struggle with anxiety and nobody knew it? Did it stem back as far as elementary school? If so, why didn't I notice when he was my student? Did he not have the tools for handling stress? What was it? Is there something we—or I—could have done differently in those years of teaching that could have better equipped him to handle life?

This is when I started to feel a responsibility. This was when I started to consider how education has changed in the past 20 years. This is when I started to think about the things that are really important to teach. For so long, we have been focused on the outcomes, but we seem to have forgotten about the process. Could our drive for better data have caused us to forget that these are just children? Have we focused too much on outcomes over process? Data over children? It's no wonder our kids have anxiety! Let's be honest, we teachers have anxiety over it too!

This train of thought and reflection led me to the big *WHAT IF*—

Introduction

What if you were told it was okay to *SLOW DOWN* in your classroom? That's not something we are used to hearing in education, right? After the initial shock of being told to slow down, I'm sure you'd have all sorts of questions, such as: "How will I meet all the standards if I slow down?" "How will they be ready for the next grade level, if I slow down?" *"How the heck am I supposed to slow down?"*

Have you ever thought about how often we tell kids to slow down? Slow down and chew your food, you could choke! Slow down, you might fall. Slow down, I can't understand what you are saying. Slow down, you're growing up too fast! Slow down and think about what you're about to do.

But do we ever tell our students to slow down while learning? I can already hear many readers saying, "WHAT?! Why would we tell our students to slow down their learning?" I'm hoping you can hear the sarcasm in my voice—but maybe not. Still, wouldn't it be great if elementary teachers were told to slow down and focus on the things that really matter?

What are those things that really matter? Several years ago, the district that I was teaching for shared with us at convocation (teacher's official first meeting) that the CEO of a large Fortune 500 Company stated they do not even care what an applicant's GPA or SAT score is. They look at three things: communication skills, ability to be a team player (collaboration), and problem-solving skills. They believed everything else on the job was teachable. These skills are developed over time and applicants seem to have them or not. This supports exactly what you will read in this book.

This book is my passion project to give teachers and administrators permission to SLOW DOWN and let these students develop the foundation they need for learning, and to equip them in the early elementary years with the proper tools for overall achievement. Now, don't get me wrong, I'm not saying we need to lessen our expectations or to lower the standards of academic rigor or achievement. What I am saying is that we can slow down in the elementary years to build a foundation for strong developmental growth. If we do this, we just might see our students blossom in a whole new way!

Teachers and administrators, we need to SLOW DOWN!

- Slow down to focus on brain development.
- Slow down to focus on developing a healthy mindset.
- Slow down to build physical strength.
- Slow down to equip our students with the tools for learning.
- Slow down to help students develop an organic desire for learning.

Ok, so who am I to give permission to slow down? Well, I am an elementary teacher who has unfortunately witnessed, over the course of a long career, what the pressure and pace of education can do to even the brightest students. I am a teacher who has spent countless hours researching child/student development and the affects developmental growth has on overall achievement. I am a teacher who used strategies for developmental growth and witnessed the difference it made in how my students began to learn and grow. I have lost sleep, as I'm sure many of you have, wondering how I will get it all done.

I am also a mom of three elementary-age kids and I see them stressing out all the time. My son is a very bright and kind kid who struggles with perfectionism. He would rather not do something at all than fail at trying. I've wiped tears over passing levels of math tests. This form of anxiety has even caused him to twirl his hair and at times, he's even pulled it out.

From what I hear, I'm not alone in this struggle. Many parents that I've talked with have witnessed the same thing with their own kids. I've spent countless hours reading about how to respond when your child says, "I'm just so stupid!" every time he messes up.

My middle daughter truly struggles with comprehension, but she works her tail off. She has worked so hard to strengthen her work-

Introduction

ing memory and continues to persist. Together we have learned what works for her. I suppose I shouldn't fail to mention my youngest daughter who is a spitfire who lacks self-control. As of the writing of this book, she has just finished her kindergarten year and has given us a run for our money. Our kids are the joy of our lives, but like all children, they each have their own unique struggles.

My research on developmental growth and use of what I've learned in my own classrooms and at home has proven to work! I have learned the importance of coaching children through the process of understanding that they are unique and are not supposed to be any particular way. I have learned that mindset and brain development will make a difference in how they view themselves. As parents we often want them to fit into a certain mold that we have created for them. As educators we focus so much on the standards set for them. But there is no mold. We just have to help build a foundation for learning, a joy for learning, and slowly allow them to develop into the person they were built to be.

I am here to share with you my experiences in the classroom and the school system at large, true stories that illustrate the need for us to slow down and which set me on the path to studying what could be done. I will also share what I have learned through primary and secondary research that supports my goal, which is to provide you with practical strategies that you can easily implement in your own classroom and will allow you to place a key focus on developmental growth.

I used to say that my job is to shape and mold the future, and of course there was humor in my voice when I said it. But isn't that what we are doing? Each day when we enter our classrooms, we're showing our students how to become what they are meant to be. We are equipping them with the tools necessary for becoming productive, kind human beings who can contribute to our society. That is exactly what we do! Yes, we teach the academic part of it, but there's so much more that has to do with each student developing as a human being, someone who wants to learn and grow and become. So yes, I shape and mold the future. And if you're reading this book, so do you!

Teachers play a major role in shaping and molding their students with the hope that they will become the best version of themselves. Does this mean that we teach them a rigorous curriculum? That we teach the standards for mastery? That we give them as much knowledge as their brains can hold? Does it mean we expect to see exponential growth from our students each year? Does it mean striving to be the best?

Yes! It means all of that, but it means so much more! Shaping and molding the future for these kids means that we help them to understand how to advocate for themselves so that they can apply effort and learn from their failures. It means providing them with the tools needed to reach their fullest potential. It means showing them what it looks like to live a healthy and productive life.

My fellow educators, consider these questions: Do you teach in a way that is preparing your students for future academic achievement? Or are you teaching them how to reach their fullest potential overall? Are you focused on the product or the process? Are you teaching standards or children?

As general education teachers, we have so much to learn about developmental growth and how it can affect a student's learning. Listen, I know we all took the classes in classroom management, pedagogy, and curriculum design, but we also know that what we learned during the small amount of student teaching and every single year in our own classrooms was far more beneficial than any class we took in college.

Education is so much more than just teaching the standards to a group and labeling them based on their academic achievement. I want this book to be a reminder that, while every grade level has different developmental milestones, the lack of a strong foundation can have long-term consequences for a child's learning. We are not only teaching the academic state standards, but we are also providing students with the opportunity to grow developmentally. This includes cognitive, emotional, and physical growth, and developing a mindset for learning. This type of growth cannot be as easily assessed, as if it was a score on a math test. In fact, child development isn't assessed unless there is a proven delay. However, all students, delay or not, need to grow developmentally. We cannot just assume that it will happen on its own.

I assumed my former student Brian was on his way to finding success. Did my assumption cause me to neglect his developmental growth? Maybe, maybe not. Were his teachers more focused on the standards or developing the students? I can't answer that, but I can tell you that we cannot just assume that every student will achieve the best outcomes unless we are able to focus on developing the whole child.

I know more now about how the brain works and how mindset can make all the difference in learning. I know now—after countless hours of research, learning strategies from specialists, and teaching alongside the building specialists in these areas—that developmental growth is the key to a student's overall achievement.

It is my hope that this book will help administrators and classroom teachers alike understand the importance of developing the whole child and equipping young learners with specific strategies for building their skills, with the goal of building a firm foundation for learning. I hope you will use this as a personal guide for implementing effective strategies for developmental growth. I want to help you feel better prepared to support your students' cognitive, physical, and emotional development.

Our school specialists have been trained to understand child development in their own area of expertise (Intervention Specialists, Occupational Therapists, Speech/Language Therapists, Guidance Counselors, Behavior Coaches, etc.). General education classroom teachers are minimally trained in these specific developmental areas and administrators, unless they were a specialist before becoming an admin, often have the same gaps in their background knowledge as classroom teachers.

I can't stress how important it is for our administrators to understand child development and this book is for them as well. So often, teachers are not given the freedom to support non-academic learning because administrators either do not understand developmental growth, or they simply place the value on academic content areas over developing the whole child. I'm hoping that reading this book will bring awareness of the need to shift our focus, especially in the primary elementary grades, to developmental growth for all learners in order to support academic achievement.

You have a powerful opportunity to support students in achieving success. That opportunity is not simply knowing how to cram as much as you can into their brain or striving to get the best scores on tests. No! What I am talking about is the powerful opportunity to shape and mold these tiny humans into who they were meant to be. They are all so uniquely designed, and our job is to develop them into what they were designed for. In order to do that, we must choose to slow down to focus on developmental growth in order for our students to become their own very best.

I can't tell you how many times I've heard administrators and colleagues of mine say, "There's no time for that silly fun stuff. We need to get our students to this point by the end of the year." But what if the silly fun stuff is exactly what they need in order to develop a strong foundation? Do they not realize that singing songs and nursery rhymes are an integral part of understanding phonemic awareness? When they peek into the room and see students playing games, do they not realize that executive function skills are at work? Or when students are playing with playdough**, do they not understand that they're working their motor skills? When they say there isn't time for more recess, do they

* Though the official name of the product sold in stores is "Play Doh," many teachers make their own "playdough." Throughout this book, I use generic names of educational tools and supplies, unless the only appropriate one to use is the branded name.

realize that recess is where and when kids learn to communicate, collaborate, solve problems, investigate, and build motor skills?

There's a lot of pressure on parents, teachers, and schools to meet academic goals. This book is a way to help reconcile some of that pressure. I just want to remind you that it's okay to slow down. Slow down and teach life skills. Slow down and teach students how to organize. Slow down and teach them to develop positive relationships and mindset. Slow down to support their mental and physical development. Slow down and focus on receptive literacy skills (e.g., listening, reading text, reading someone's signed words) and expressive language (e.g., speaking, telling a story). Slow down to focus on your students' organic curiosities. Do you get my point?

Somehow, somewhere, we created this race to academic achievement that has become unhealthy for so many. Let's look at some areas that are worth slowing down in order to focus on creating mentally, emotionally, and physically healthy students who can handle the rigor of their education.

We can shape and mold the future by helping our students become well-rounded human beings. We can equip our students with tools for handling all that is thrown at them.

I want to share all the strategies I've learned through the years of working with specialists. *Slow Down! Children are Learning!* is written in three sections:

- *In Part One*, I lay out the argument for why teachers should spend time on developmental skills and the benefits of a strong foundation. I share stories from my own life and career that illustrate how anxiety and the fear of failing affects students and how they learn. I also map out a framework for building a firm foundation for learning.

- *In Part Two,* I dig deep into different areas of developmental growth and provide examples of practical strategies—little moves we can make in our classrooms—that I have learned from working so closely with the Educational Specialists. Each chapter in this section will explain a separate developmental area—what it is, why it is important, and how to implement it in the classroom.
- *Last, Part Three* discusses several different educational pedagogies that are proven to be developmentally appropriate for learning. These are bigger moves that we make because they are more about how we teach and often require us to pivot from what we are used to.

So here we go! Let's slow down and be the difference in the learning experience of our students! I want you to realize—like REALLY realize—that what you do each day in your classroom matters! The silly fun stuff matters. The songs and stories matter. The time you take to share your own personal stories matters. Taking time to build relationships matters! I want you to realize that you—yes, YOU—can be the difference in how your students achieve success. Let's start by just slowing down!

PART ONE

Are We Teaching Standards, or Are We Teaching Humans?

When I first started teaching there was a teacher assigned to be my mentor. She was only a couple of years away from her retirement and she would often share memories of her favorite units to teach her 3rd graders. She had a passion for teaching kids. Did you catch that? Kids. She had a passion for teaching children to learn and grow. As a brand-new teacher who was taught all about the importance of teaching the mandated state standards, I watched her struggle to follow along with this new way of planning, instructing, and assessing. The year she retired, she announced to our team that she planned to teach the way she knew was best for kids; she planned to teach the units that she knew kids enjoyed the most. She was confident she would still get in the standards she was responsible for. Basically, she was going rogue!

You see, my mentor teacher knew something I did not know at the time (or maybe I knew it, but just didn't think about it). She knew that teaching kids was more important than teaching standards. That is exactly what the first section of this book is about. I will share real life stories of how our focus on high achievement of standards has caused immense anxiety for both teachers and students, and stories of how our focus on every child mastering every academic standard has taken away the organic love of learning—along with creating very little time in the day to build relationships, teach empathy, and equip our students with the proper tools and mindset for success.

This first section will explain the importance of establishing a strong foundation for learning. Elementary school is where we build that strong foundation. We cannot rush our way through that or skip ahead to get all those mandated standards taught.

The first section will share my framework for building a FIRM foundation for learning. A firm foundation is the base for all things of value: structures, relationships, human character, and academics. Deep down we all know this! Administrators, teachers, parents—all of us know that a firm foundation for anything is necessary.

It's funny that 20 years ago, my mentor teacher, along with other veteran teachers, would tell us new teachers that we would eventually witness the philosophy of teaching come full circle. Out with the old, in with the new, until the old comes back again. I will never forget that. In fact, what I have learned through my research for this book is that some of those "old philosophies of teaching" were actually right on track for building a firm foundation for learning. We know more now than ever before and now we have the research to prove it! So before we dive in, let me ask you, "Are you teaching standards or are you teaching humans?"

CHAPTER 1

Fear of Failing

Over the last two decades, I've watched our education system take a turn from focusing on the learner to focusing on standardized test results and data. This turn has been both positive and negative. I see the turn beginning with the No Child Left Behind Act of 2002. It gave educators nationwide focus and accountability, but it also created a race for school districts to be rated the best, and the resulting pressure put on teachers to achieve results unfortunately shifted the focus from the child to the test. Looking back, I can see that this has placed the type of pressure on our students that has created a whole new problem for learners—anxiety.

As I learned more about Brian's story, I realized that during his elementary years, education was focusing on standardized test data and academic outcomes. Parents and students were told in advance that they would not go on to the next grade if they didn't pass the test. This is still true in many states' education systems today. After speaking with Brian's mom and hearing her perspective of his situation, I learned that everyone viewed Brian as confident, compassionate, and a hard worker. The story of what he faced during his freshman year in college illustrates what anxiety and depression can do to a young person trying to find success.

This success that everyone speaks of is what really overwhelmed Brian—all of the tests, all of college prep, and lots of worries about not knowing what direction he wanted to take in college. Brian told me that leaving the normalcy of school-age life and heading into the unknown new college life was a lot to handle. He became weighed down with the stress of the idea of one day having to support a family, and still not knowing what he wanted to do. Even though his family provided him with great advice, love, and support, Brian continued to feel this stress. Big tasks started to seem impossible, and it was difficult to break them down. It was as though he didn't have the mental tools needed to break down the big task into smaller tasks. Even packing his lunch became a struggle, because that was a reminder that another day was ahead, and he didn't want to face it.

Brian and his family had discussed this periodically, but they felt as though he was just battling regular teenage worries, as many kids face. Brian was speaking with a counselor on a regular basis. This seemed to be helping him. It was this counselor who probably saved his life. She called Brian's mom and asked her to come get him immediately, after hearing that Brian was in fact considering self-harm.

This reality that Brian and his family had to face just about wrecked me. It troubled me because I know this wonderful family. I know that he was raised right. I know that he was loved and supported. So, I couldn't wrap my head around why he would choose this.

Chapter 1: Fear of Failing

Thinking About Today's Brians

As I continued to think about Brian and the third-grader I knew him as in my class, I remembered him doubting himself a bit when he was in 3rd grade. I wondered if, although from the outside he seemed to have it all together, on the inside he struggled with self-esteem. I then started to realize that my own son, Cooper, who was in 3rd grade at the time, was a lot like Brian. Cooper had extreme test anxiety, although his teachers probably couldn't tell. He was a bit of a perfectionist. In fact, he would rather not try at all than try and fail. Many kids think failing at something or not being perfect is simply a failed ending. If only they realized that with some effort, they will succeed! Why do they get so overwhelmed when they aren't perfect? Why are they so afraid to fail? Because we said so! We (adults in their lives) have told our students that they have to pass the tests. We have given them a tall order—achieve or else! The good news is that we can change this so that these kids will have the confidence, persistence, and courage to fail and try again, and fail, and try again.

How can we teach them that the failures are how we learn? At this point, I think you all probably feel the same as I do. Of course, we want to make a difference for them! Of course, we want to slow down and reduce their anxiety. The big question is, how do we do that? We need to have our administrators on board with this shift of thinking. We need our elementary teachers to be willing to slow down and trust that it will get our students ahead in the long run.

I feel an extreme amount of responsibility to teach my own son the proper tools for being an effective learner, a responsibility to train his brain to see failure as a learning experience. This responsibility is not just on me as a parent, but also on me as a teacher. I want to make a difference in education! I want to help the decision-makers in the world of education see the importance of the early learning years. I want teachers to feel as though they are given permission to shift their focus to developmental areas that are not measured on state tests. This is where we teachers can be the big difference.

Every student needs more explicit instruction in the developmental areas that contribute to a firm foundation for learning. Every student deserves to learn how to develop their brain in a way that will support their journey through education. In my years of teaching, I didn't really understand all of this until I started teaching in an inclusive classroom, where the students who were on IEPs (Individualized Education Plans) stayed in the classroom and the specialists came to them. This provided me with the opportunity to co-teach with the specialists in our building. It wasn't until then that I learned how to teach lessons to develop the executive function skills or to help the students develop a growth mindset. I also learned that working at a slower pace allows the brain to better access the information learned and use it to function in the classroom.

We haven't been focusing on social-emotional learning and yet, we need to make that a priority. Up until now, schools have wanted the data to show high achievement. I have wondered why we so often just assume that the regular education students will figure it all out on their own. The academic data does not give us the whole picture when it comes to what and how a student learns and develops. In fact, sometimes it's the Average Joe (or Brian in this case), who slips through the cracks or is not noticed, or could have handled the pressure, had we focused more on developmental growth during the early elementary years.

Looking back, I think Brian's story could have been different if we knew then what we know now about the brain and about development. It's impossible to know for sure, but I believe that if the focus on Brian's early education was developmental growth, providing him with the tools for learning rather than on achieving the outcomes, he may have been better equipped for what lay ahead in his educational career.

Shifting the Paradigm and Addressing Anxiety

The high demands, unrelenting pace, and academic difficulty have caused a problem of its own—anxiety. According to a survey done by the Pew Research Center in 2019, anxiety and depression rates are on the rise. The survey found that 61% of teens say that achieving good grades is the main source of the day-to-day pressure they face. School leaders, educators, and parents can help to fix this by understanding the importance of developmental growth. We need to understand that it is up to us to provide our students with the tools they need to handle the pressure they will experience as they progress each year.

I believe that we can reduce anxiety in students if we choose to place more focus on these fundamental areas. When children enter kindergarten, they are often given a label based on what they know or don't know. We often ask them to ignore their natural desire to play and be curious. Instead, we ask them to sit still and listen. They come into kindergarten often unable to hold a pencil and form letters, and yet they are expected to write a five-sentence paragraph by the end of that same year. Seriously, I have anxiety for them just thinking about it!

If our students are already feeling stressed about learning in kindergarten, how will they feel in 3rd grade when the learning begins to get more complex? Larry Steinberg, a university professor of psychology and author of *Age of Opportunity: Lessons from the New Science of Adolescence*, explains why regulating emotions is difficult in the years between childhood and adulthood. He shares that many kids are maturing physically earlier than the brain develops emotionally and intellectually. This can create a perfect storm for failures of self-control and emotional regulation. To this point, I've learned that we need to teach our students strategies that will prepare them to be the authority of their own self-control.

These aren't new problems, but they are problems that teacher education programs don't always prepare us for. As we learn more about the brain, we can better equip our students with the right tools for these problems. Having a strong foundation to build on is the first step. Providing them with tools and strategies that will allow them to handle the added stress of middle school and juggle all that comes with being in high school will be key. How will they handle being an adult when they have felt anxious ever since they started school back in kindergarten? There will still be young people who struggle with anxiety and fears, but I believe there are things we can do to help fight that battle alongside of them.

By the time students get to 3rd grade when the learning begins to get more complex, we have often failed to provide them with the appropriate mental, emotional, and physical tools to handle the complexity and rigor of academics. They are not confident in their own abilities because there is little time to stop and celebrate the little accomplishments along the way, like self-control, effort, persistence, and taking the time to have conversations about failures. They instead have had to focus on learning, testing, and remediation until mastery is formed. They have had to keep plugging away.

Frankly, I feel stressed out just thinking back to those days teaching 3rd grade. The stress was not good for anyone involved. The funny thing is, I don't think I even realized it then. I didn't see it, until I experienced my own son's anxiety and later heard about Brian's story. Then it hit me, and I could see clearly what the system has been doing to kids and educators alike.

It was a well-oiled machine where I came from. The kids moved on academically year after year, teachers planned to teach, assess, re-teach, assess, etc. The district I was teaching for had the data to prove that our process was working. Our kids achieved academically, and we had the data to prove it! But looking back, I wish we would have realized the impact that a focus on developmental areas has on overall achievement. You see, there was little time to spend on relational skills, organizational skills, and communication skills. It's not that we didn't work on those things at all, but our focus was definitely on passing the test and getting the data. In hindsight, I can see how much was by lost by placing our focus on the product over the process.

During these years of standards-based teaching is when Brian was in my class and I could see it faintly causing him stress, now that I think back on those days. Brian achieved academic success and more. But it was stressing him out. It saddens me that during those years, our focus on academic data left us with little time for developing an organic love for learning.

More recently, I experienced having my own child go through the stress and anxiety of taking standardized tests. My friend's son Danny is the same age as my son. He does not struggle academically. He is a hard worker, and his hard work pays off. Danny cares deeply about making those around him proud. He is a bit sensitive, especially if he thinks he's disappointed others. His teacher told their class, "If you don't pass this test, you will not get to move on to the next grade!" Danny went home and had a complete meltdown over this. He cried for hours and would not listen to anything his mother was saying. He continued to cry as his mom told him that "The test doesn't matter. He'll do fine, and it's just a test." Deep down, Danny didn't believe his mom. If his teacher said he had to pass, then he had to pass!

At the same school, a different teacher told her class, "Don't stress! This test is no big deal." She let the kids know that all they needed to do was their own personal best. She focused on the effort rather than the results. I know this because my own son, Cooper, was in her class. Cooper is typically a ball of stress when it comes to tests, but not this time. His teacher's message was just what he needed to help him focus on his effort rather than his score on the test.

You see, kids believe what their teachers say! Danny would not believe his mom when she said that the test didn't matter. But what his teacher said stuck in his mind. *"If you don't pass the test, you won't move on to the next grade."* The result was stress and anxiety for Danny. My own son, on the other hand, didn't stress a bit over his test. He could hear his teacher in his mind saying, *"Just do your best, it's not a big deal."*

Which teacher would you want your child to have? What kind of teacher are you? As educators we must really think about what we say and how we say it to our students. They do listen to us! They want to please us! Our perspective and attitude can have an enormous impact on the perspectives that our students form about learning.

YOU Can Be Their Difference!

Dr. Margie Gillis, a nationally recognized literacy expert and a Certified Academic Language Therapist, was quoted in an article titled "Taking Back Kindergarten: Rethinking Rigor for Young Learners," by Dr. Sarah K. Silverman. Dr. Gillis stated that,

> Developmentally appropriate instruction in Kindergarten is about striking the right balance between ensuring that Kindergarten age children are exposed to big ideas and vocabulary, and also understand how to self-regulate. Children can thrive in a classroom that intentionally develops their ability to function within a learning environment, and that also exposes them to ideas, concepts, vocabulary, and opportunities for language expression and development.

I believe that at any grade level we can provide our students with the proper tools for handling themselves in a way that will ensure success! In the next chapter, I'll provide more context about explicitly teaching children to function in a classroom. We will learn how to shift the paradigm of what and how we teach. I'm here to remind you that it's not about test results, rather human results. Steve Zwolak, CEO of Loom Institute and Executive Director of

Chapter 1: Fear of Failing

University City Children's Center, says that all behavior has meaning and that we need to spend time working through behaviors with our students. Zwolak states, "We need to stop teaching the head and teach the soul." We may have had it right all those years ago when kindergarteners still had rest time, play time, free and imaginative play, and plenty of field trips. Today we are taking away the element of imagination and fun and replacing it with complex academics.

It's hard. There are a lot of conflicting pressures. However, we can shift our focus from academics to developmental growth in the early years, so that our students can be better equipped with the tools needed to find success in upper grades. I'm not saying that we shouldn't have a rigorous academic system. On the contrary, I think that every student should be challenged to be better each day. However, working to be better each day will look different for every student at every grade level. I believe that we need to teach not only the standards, but the tools our students will need in order to conquer the standards. We need to make this shift in order for our students to develop physically, emotionally, and cognitively.

A paradigm shift is defined as "an important change that happens when the usual way of thinking about or doing something is replaced by a new and different way." My theory is that if we slow down in elementary school and shift our focus to the developmental needs of the kids we teach, then we can more easily maintain a rigorous curriculum throughout their school years. If we do this, if we slow down and focus on the right things, then when the time comes, these students will hit their learning targets and move forward as physically, emotionally, and mentally healthy lifelong learners.

Who wants to be a teacher who develops an effective and productive human who is able to handle what is thrown at them? I think you do. I know I do! So, join me. I hope you enjoy learning practical strategies for slowing down to get ahead by shifting the paradigm from racing to the top academically, to placing the focus on the developmental growth of our students.

CHAPTER 2

Who's Afraid of the Big Bad Wolf? Building a Foundation for Learning

We all know the story of the Three Little Pigs. Of course, we've heard it throughout our lives and we know that the house carefully made of bricks is the one strong enough to keep the Big Bad Wolf out! We also know that the other pigs finished their houses quickly and moved on to other things—until, of course, the Big Bad Wolf came and blew their houses down.

In the beginning stages of building their houses, the first two little pigs were proud and excited about completing their houses. They had their finished product and had time for other things, while the third pig plugged away, carefully placing each brick to make a strong foundation. You see, the pig building the house of bricks didn't care that his house was taking longer. He didn't change what he knew was important because the others were getting what looked like immediate results. No, the third little pig knew that taking the time to build a strong foundation would get him even better end results. He knew that reaching the end goal fastest may not actually save him from the Big Bad Wolf. The time he invested at the beginning, building the bricks for his strong home, paid off! As we know, it also saved the other two pigs.

This book is your pile of bricks, and you are the third little pig taking time to be intentional about laying the foundation for each of your students. We can take our time developing a foundation for learning before we ever worry about a detail in the state standards. Just as the third pig carefully laid each brick with mortar, we too need to lay a foundation that will support the learning process for each student.

Sometimes I think that we classroom teachers just need permission to slow down and teach what really matters. We all know what is really important, but we are not sure we have permission to follow those instincts. So, I am going to be bold and give you that permission. If you are reading this book—permission granted! Deep down we know that we cannot expect our students to learn all the academic standards without first building a firm foundation for learning. We must take time at the beginning to carefully place the developmental "bricks" so that our students will soar in the long run. For more than a decade we've been placing our focus on progressing through the academic standards and test-taking strategies. I often think we need to hear that it's okay and necessary to slow down. We need our administrators to understand this and to encourage it. We also need to have our grade level teams on board. Then we can gather the materials and study the process for building this foundation.

This is where I can help! I will share with you how to implement strategies that I've learned throughout my years of teaching. These developmental strategies will develop your students into well-rounded humans who love to learn and have the mental tools to do so. I will walk you through each developmental area and explain how I used it in my own classrooms to build strong learners. We will carefully lay that foundation for learning that will provide your students with the tools necessary for success in learning. I will share effective share strategies to use with your students.

What Are Foundational Skills for Learning?

Foundational skills are the building blocks that allow students to successfully learn and grow. Building up strong foundational skills will allow students to grasp new concepts more easily. The

National Educational Goals Panel published articles explaining the five essential areas of school readiness. When they talk about school readiness, they are referring to students being ready to start kindergarten. This is the optimal time to build a firm foundation for learning. However, with every new school year, we need to take time to revisit and build upon our firm foundations for learning. These essential areas for building a firm foundation include:

- Social and emotional development
- Cognition and general knowledge
- Communication: language and literacy
- Physical development and health
- Approaches that develop a natural curiosity to learn

All of these areas begin to develop in the first five years of life. Development during these years is crucial to our kids' success throughout their school career. Although the public schools are not always part of the first five years of a child's life, we still need a starting point when they do enter kindergarten. Because our students come from diverse backgrounds and settings, we must be intentional about developing this strong foundation for our students' future success. According to the National Association for the Education of Young Children (NAEYC), behavioral research establishes relationships between play and development in several areas: language and literacy, executive function skills, mathematics and spatial skills, scientific thinking, and social and emotional development. These skills are fundamentals. They are essential to learning in school and in life.

Chapter 2: Building a Foundation for Learning

During my years of teaching inclusive classrooms, I was given the opportunity to co-teach with many of our building specialists. What I learned during this time was that the very specific strategies that they were using with their identified students were strategies that every student in my class was benefiting from.

- *Special Education* teachers taught me how to modify lessons to ensure every student in my classroom found success.
- *Speech and Language Pathologists* modeled how to support students' communication, self-regulation, organization, and other executive function skills.
- *Occupational Therapists* taught me specific strategies for motor development, handwriting, and sensory integration to use in my classroom.
- *Physical Therapists* worked one-on-one with students who had specific physical limitations and/or deficits.
- *Audiologists* provided the proper tools and taught me how to use them with hearing-impaired students in my class, and helped me to teach lessons to my class about better understanding and accepting hearing impairments.
- *School Counselors* worked closely with me to design lessons that incorporated mindset, social-emotional learning, and strategies for behavior management.
- *Reading Specialists* supported me in assessing students' reading levels and provided strategies to use for teaching literacy skills.

These specialists were slowly teaching the essentials for building a learning foundation. Obviously, there isn't enough time in the day for every student to learn from these specialists, so I tried to learn as much as I could. I asked lots of questions and, although their primary responsibility wasn't to me, they were a great resource to learn from. They understood, and helped me understand, students' particular needs because they understood students' particular needs in ways we classroom teachers don't. These specialists are just that—specialized! The knowledge that I gained from working so closely with these specialists was tremendous. I learned things that were never taught to me in college. Together we used the strategies they knew worked for their students with my whole class. And these strategies are what I want to share with you.

Why Are Foundational Skills Important?

I think we can all agree that a strong foundation—for anything, really! —is vital. I mean, do you want your house to be blown down by the Big Bad Wolf? Building a firm foundation is essential for the success that our students will find throughout their life. When we focus on these areas in order to form our foundation for learning, every year, every grade, every advancement in their education will build upon this foundation.

Think about your own classroom. How do you support foundational skills? What do you want to know more about? It's more than teaching kids to read, it's teaching kids to be able to handle learning how to read. It's understanding how their brains work and knowing how to develop them to support their learning. These specialists were teaching the essentials for building a firm foundation for learning. I started wondering why regular education students with no delays were not given the opportunity to work with these specialists.

We know that the foundations for learning begin to develop in the early childhood years. However, in the beginning elementary years, we must take added time to be intentional about implementing these foundational learning skills. How well their foundational skills have been developed will determine how they grasp new concepts. All children develop at different rates. That said, when a child enters elementary school (typically in kindergarten), they come to us with a variety of experiences that have shaped who they are, what they know, and their developmental state. In kindergarten through 2nd grade, we must focus on ensuring these foundational skills are firmly in place.

I have witnessed students being pushed through the curriculum and expressing frustration because they weren't physically, mentally, and/or emotionally ready for what was being asked of them. Quite frankly, without consciously working on developing these needs in our students, we cannot expect them to achieve academically. They will be running from the Big Bad Wolf, just like the first two little pigs. It is our job as educators to make sure that our kids have a firm foundation for learning. When these foundations for learning are developed, nurtured, and enriched each year as they come to us, students will be more likely to take academic risks, and to become leaders and innovators. This means that in the beginning years of elementary school, we need to set aside time in our day for lessons and activities that will promote developmental growth.

We cannot afford to rush through building this foundation for learning. We must learn from the old fable of the little pigs! Spending time building a strong firm foundation for learning is the most important thing you can do in teaching. We cannot get wrapped up in our long list of standards and rushing to get them mastered, only to move on to the next. No, we need to let these foundations become habits, practicing them until they are concrete, rock hard, never failing. If we spend more time frontloading, carefully developing the foundation, in the end we gain even more success! I know, I know, I keep saying the same thing over and over—but it's because it's that important! You see, we can learn a lot from the three little pigs. Which little pig will your students be like? Will they get it done quickly and move on? Or will they take time to build the concrete solid foundation they need? I'm pretty sure I know your answer! Who's afraid of the Big Bad Wolf now?

How to Build a Strong Foundation for Learning

Elementary Education is the foundation. It has to start at the beginning! How do we do it? What resources and materials do we use? Well, we do it nice and slow, developing the whole child. We ask questions from the specialists in our building. We acknowledge the fact that primary age kids have different developmental needs. We reflect on our own classroom environment and instruction. We also observe student behavior and ability. When we understand our students, we can then reflect on how our classroom environment and instruction can support our students' developmental needs. We are role models for behavior and attitude, and we model strategies that will help our learners. We provide opportunities for our students to celebrate the little accomplishments. We teach them about having a positive mindset.

The younger we develop the whole child, the stronger their foundation for learning will be. This means that if you teach elementary school, building their foundation for learning is essential! This is not just for kindergarten—this is for all elementary grades. You will set the tone for their perspective of learning. The way that you teach and what you teach will determine how students perceive themselves as learners, people, teammates, and leaders.

A firm foundation is the first step in academic achievement.This doesn't mean that you're off the hook if you are a middle school teacher, high school teacher, or administrator. No, you have work to do as well. As our kids grow, we must continue to build and strengthen our students mentally, physically, and emotionally. We must begin each year, each semester, each day, with setting a positive foundation for learning.

We can teach in a way that focuses on developmental skills. As we work toward developmental growth, our students will become confident, independent, and engaged learners. Developmental skills become the framework for a firm foundation for learning.

Chapter 2: Building a Foundation for Learning

When we nurture these skills, we will find that students are more likely to be motivated, have purpose, and be engaged in a way that creates a love for learning and a drive to learn more, leading to academic achievement and overall success.

Overall success will look different for each student. It's no secret that children all develop at a different rate. In fact, I always thought it interesting that when you have a baby, you get monthly updates from your doctor about the new developmental milestones that you can expect. Of course, there's always the disclaimer mentioning that all children develop at a different rate, and common sense and experience confirms this is true. But what really gets me is that when children enter kindergarten, all of the sudden they are all expected to be "kindergarteners," all at about the same level of development. Well, what happened to every child developing at a different rate?

When it comes to development, there are many variabilities. Developmental growth is not a smooth straight line, regardless of whether a child has a disability or not. Every student will advance at a different rate and in different areas. You and I both know that the system isn't perfect. We also know that teachers work very hard to differentiate in order to meet the needs of all students. However, sometimes things that impact a student's progress are out of our control. This, by the way, doesn't mean you haven't done enough. This is why we choose to lean in and learn from the specialists. This is why we choose to continue to try new strategies. This is also why, when you teach in the early grade levels, we must choose to focus on what we can control.

It doesn't matter what grade or subject that you teach. You must first establish a foundation for learning in your class. What does that look like? Well, we can start with the word FIRM, as in Firm Foundation. Our foundation will be built F. I. R. M. with Functionality, Inquiring Minds, Relationships, and Mindset. In a nutshell, before you ever teach an academic standard (though some of these skills can be found in your state or national standards), you will commit to teaching your students how to function in your class and at school. You will also create a space that leaves your students curious to know more. You will show them how to build relationships with others and how to communicate. In addition, you will work to develop a positive mindset for both yourself and your students. You can set the tone by showing them that you believe in them and that they too will believe in themselves. This, my friends, is the beginning of building a FIRM foundation for your students learning. Let's dig deeper into this!

F	Functionality
I	Inquiring minds
R	Relationships
M	Mindset

Functionality

Teaching your students how to function as productive learners within your classroom is so important! Some of your students may have an IEP and the support from a Speech/Language Pathologist, Intervention Specialists, or Guidance Counselor to help them navigate their day. I want to show you how to support your whole class in a similar way. I've learned from my own experience during my time teaching with these specialists that every student can benefit from such support. Slowly modeling how to use strategies that will help them function in your class will make a huge difference in how they achieve.

In order for a student to function with ease, you will want to spend ample time on the following aspects of functionality:
- Processes and Procedures
- Expectations
- Organization

- Listening and Speaking
- Perspective and Attitude
- Contributing to the Greater Good

Oftentimes we assume that our students will just figure these things out. The truth is, though, that when we take the time to teach, model, observe, correct, and instruct specific skills, they are more able to function successfully in the classroom. For example, the first week of school is when we all set up our expectations and get to know each other. I take a whole day or, for some, a whole week just to get the class organized, acquainted with the space, acquainted with each other, and learning what is going to be expected. We have to take time to do this slowly and intentionally. Taking the time to teach functionality will be worth it, as your students will be more likely to go about their day effectively and efficiently.

Being able to function effectively and efficiently has a lot to do with understanding who we are. We can teach our students to identify and understand how they think and feel, what they like and dislike, what makes them happy or sad, and what their strengths and weaknesses are. Depending on their age and their experiences prior to being in your class, you may even have the opportunity and responsibility of teaching your students effective ways to respond to how they think or feel in different situations.

Being able to function in the classroom requires respect, responsibility, and a sense of priority. Your students' mindsets and developmental abilities will also play a role in their day-to-day functionality. There is power in understanding what kind of learner you are. There is power in understanding what makes you angry, sad, or experiencing any other emotion. There is great power in understanding how to respond to what you need. When students see they are able to advocate for themselves, have control over their emotions, or choose to make the right decisions, they will be able to function more effectively and efficiently.

As we plan for our day-to-day lessons and activities, we must plan to teach our students how to function independently. We can teach them how to function in the classroom by teaching them how to follow a process or a to-do list. We can also teach them how to be organized and provide them with the proper tools to do so. We can teach them how a student functions in a large group or in a small group. We can teach them to advocate for themselves.

You see, we so often just assume that our students will figure out how to function. But the truth is, when we show them exactly how to do it, then we no longer have to hope they will figure it out on their own. Teaching your students how to function will set them up for success. When students can be active participants in the functionality of the learning environment, FIRM foundations for learning are built!

Inquiring Minds

Part of building this FIRM foundation for learning is creating a space for curiosity. Does your class have any mysteries in it? Do your students leave each day wanting to come back? There are so many ways to make learning fun and exciting. Kids are curious by nature. We need to take their curiosity and run with it! This might mean changing our original plan. This might mean taking a broad learning standard and letting the students curiosity lead the learning. This might also mean changing the scenery. You can relocate your lesson, alter the classroom setting, set up a stage, dress in costume to fit the topic, just to name a few suggestions. There are so many ways to get our students excited about discovering what needs to be learned.

One teacher friend of mine, Mrs. C., has always had a classroom pet. No matter the grade level, a classroom pet can teach so much. When she walked into her room one morning, her hamster was gone! She couldn't find it anywhere. She considered making up a story so that the kids wouldn't be upset when they got to school and noticed the hamster missing. But time got away from her and before she knew it, the kids were entering the classroom. When the students noticed, she decided that honesty was the best policy. The kids were sad for a second, until one student suggests that it has to be somewhere. *Let's find it!*

The teacher stopped her original plan and conducted a class meeting. The students brainstormed ideas for how to find the hamster. First, they decided to have a "search party," looking all over the classroom. When this failed, they decided they would spread the word outside of their classroom walls. They made "Lost Hamster" posters to hang around the school. Mrs. C. tried to move on in her day with her regular lesson plans, but the students simply could not drop the idea of locating the lost hamster. She took this opportunity to let her class do a little research. They discovered what hamsters like to eat and researched their character and habitat.

This continued on through the day, leading to lengthy lessons on simple machines. By the end of the week, Mrs. C. class knew all about incline planes, levers, pulleys, wheels, and so on. The students took what they learned to lure the hamster back to its cage. They placed its favorite snack in the cage, with a trail of snacks leading to it. They created a maze of sorts with materials from around the room so that when the hamster found the snack trail it had to follow it. They created a trap inside the cage so that the hamster couldn't get back out.

This teacher's lesson plans for the week didn't go as planned. However, her students were so motivated to come to school and figure this out. They worked so hard to achieve the goal of finding the lost hamster. They benefited tremendously through collaboration, planning, organizing, researching, problem solving, building, and creating.

You better believe the kids were excited to come to class each day. You better believe they were motivated and excited to figure all of that out. But what I see as the best part is that Mrs. C. set a tone for her class the minute she dropped her plan and ran with her student's curiosity. Her students learned that their teacher would support and promote learning through their inquiring minds.

Are you wondering if they ever found the hamster? Well, let's just say the kids did find the hamster back in its cage when they got to school at the end of the week. But only Mrs. C. knows that the mystery of the lost hamster actually went unsolved.

In what ways do you plan for curiosity? Are you willing to veer away from your lesson plans like the teacher in this story did? Do you take time each day to just let your students talk about what is on their minds? Are you in a rush to get your lesson plans done?

There's so much to learn from the inquiring minds of your students. Keep your students inquiring about what they want to know and what is required of them to learn. Inquiry is a foundational skill that will lead to learning so much! We want to establish a learning environment that allows and promotes curiosity. When students express that they are interested or curious about it, find a way to integrate that curiosity into the themes that you are responsible to cover.

I know the stress that is on educators to get the standards taught and mastered. Why not teach them through inquiry? Many schools have instructional coaches that help with creating hands-on and engaging units of study. Many teachers have experimented with different educational pedagogies, but I challenge you to try to use your student's natural curiosity to build upon the standard that your grade level is responsible for teaching. Present your topic and pose questions, let the students ask questions and share what they know about a given topic. Encourage them to continue asking more. Provide resources for diving deep into research to get the answers. Read stories, create models, make the learning meaningful.

The whole point of inquiry is to show our students how to solve a problem or how to get an answer. It will teach them that they learn from failing and then trying something new. It will show them that you care about what they want to learn. It will also create an organic love for learning. Developing the inquiring mind is essential to building the foundation for learning.

Relationships

Get to know your students! Learn what motivates them, what makes them happy, what scares them, what upsets them, learn it all. Invest in their lives. Show up at their baseball games, ask them how their evening was. Be intentional about giving students time to share what is on their mind. Be there for them. Build the relationship!

Getting to know your students is one of the best things that you can do, and you can get to know your students in many ways. Oftentimes elementary teachers do a Getting to Know You Board, or Star Student, or play fun games in order to learn about each other. We can learn to know our students by listening to them. Hear what they have to say. Allow for time to discuss what is on their minds. Ask their families about what makes them happy, what makes them sad, what their interests are. Invest in them!

Building Relationships is a foundational skill that will support the student throughout their educational career. It will enable them to work cooperatively in teams, with partners, and as a whole group. Learning to understand how to communicate and build relationships is something that will take them very far in life. In fact, many companies want to know that they can count on their employees to collaborate and solve problems together. Building relationships and helping students build their relationships will teach empathy and trust. It will build their confidence in who they are and how they learn. Building healthy relationships is a fundamental skill that must be modeled and taught.

Mindset

From the minute your kids enter your class, they need to know that you believe in them and that they must believe in themselves. You can start this process by teaching them about attitude and effort. A positive attitude will change the way you learn! Teach them that there is NO FEAR OF FAILING! Set the tone from day one so that your students are willing to take academic and creative risks. The best way to do this is by modeling it. Model what it looks like to learn from mistakes. Share with them a time when you failed and tried again. Talk about how everyone makes mistakes and that we learn from the mistakes we make. Celebrate when a student can share something they learned from making a mistake. This idea of mistakes being an opportunity in disguise might be the most important thing you teach your students. How they view themselves as a learner will make or break them. Their perspective of learning will shape how they learn and achieve.

We can build this foundation for learning. I'm calling all elementary educators to strive to shift their focus to building firm foundations for academic achievement. We do this by focusing on developmental growth. This means continuing to teach those standards by pulling back, slowing down, and allowing these foundational skills to become habitual. We can pull back by setting aside time to focus on the essentials that we just discussed using the acronym F.I.R.M.

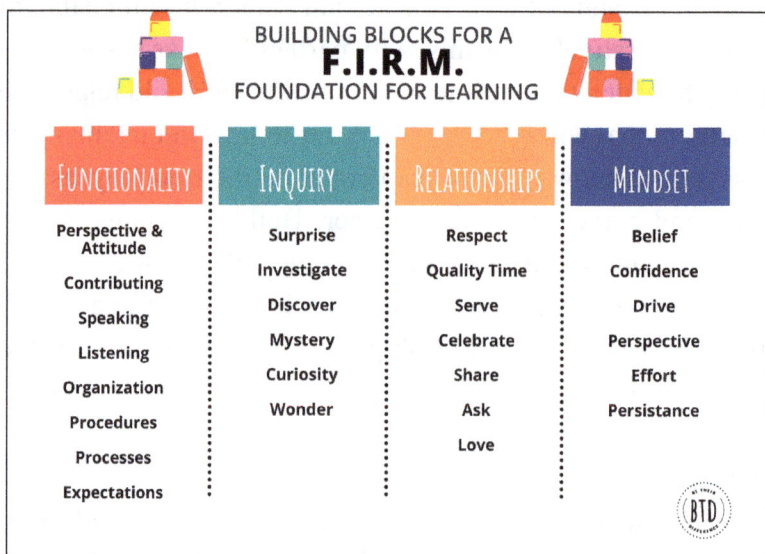

BUILDING BLOCKS FOR A
F.I.R.M.
FOUNDATION FOR LEARNING

Functionality	Inquiry	Relationships	Mindset
Perspective & Attitude	Surprise	Respect	Belief
Contributing	Investigate	Quality Time	Confidence
Speaking	Discover	Serve	Drive
Listening	Mystery	Celebrate	Perspective
Organization	Curiosity	Share	Effort
Procedures	Wonder	Ask	Persistance
Processes		Love	
Expectations			

BTD

I recently read that in the past 20 years, we've learned more about the brain than ever before. We know more about how and when it develops. We know more about how we can literally change our brain. There are practical strategies that will develop parts of the brain that will help our students. When we understand the brain and how it develops, we can then foster learning through developing the whole child. We know more today, so we need to do more today, and it should be our mission to use this knowledge to foster learning.

Developmental growth is the foundation for learning and achievement.

It's time to prioritize and really think about what will get our students prepared for the life that they will be living and the education they will be receiving. The race to academic achievement (especially in the early years) is stunting the ability of our kids to develop a love for learning, a sense of confidence and purpose, and achievement in the process of learning rather than the result. Yes, goal-setting and achieving are necessary and good! Yes, we want our kids to achieve their goals. But first we need to build a strong foundation for learning. We want to develop our youth to be confident, smart, independent, effective, and productive human beings. We want our kids to stop fearing failure and face it head on so that they can continue to grow. We can teach our kids that failing is part of the learning process!

So, how do we achieve this goal? When we focus on developmental growth, the achievement will follow! The following are areas of developmental growth that we now know have a great effect on how students behave and perform academically. I will help you be intentional about implementing the instruction of these six key skills into your classrooms:

1. Executive Function Skills
2. Growth Mindset
3. Motor Skills
4. Handwriting
5. Sensory Integration
6. Foundational Literacy Skills

Focusing on these developmental areas in your elementary classrooms will better equip your students with the proper tools for learning and will foster a love, confidence, and drive for our students to really work to their highest potential. It will also give your students the power to advocate for themselves and build on their personal strengths. Part Two of this book will explain the "what," "why," and "how" to implement these six developmental tools in your classroom to support your student's physical, social-emotional, and mental ability to learn and succeed.

AREAS OF DEVELOPMENTAL GROWTH

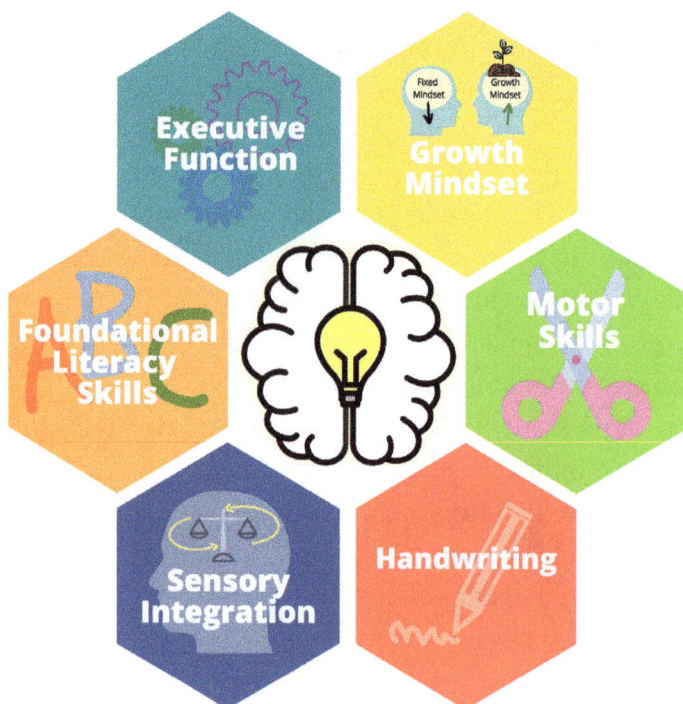

PART TWO

Little Moves: Practical Strategies for Developmental Growth in Your Classroom

This part of the book will give you knowledge, practical strategies, and the motivation to slow down to focus on specific areas of developmental growth, so that each and every student has the opportunity to grow cognitively, emotionally, and physically. Consider this section to be a tool that will help you understand the importance of slowing down in the early elementary years to focus on teaching kids how to function, how to explore and discover, how to build healthy relationships and self-confidence, and how to develop a positive mindset. When you choose to slow down to focus on these skills, your students will benefit in the long run.

In the first section, I established the importance of building a FIRM foundation for learning. Building a strong foundation is the key to anything, really, and now you will learn how to build on that foundation. Part Two is dedicated to sharing with you the knowledge and strategies that I learned from the specialists that worked with me throughout my career. You will see that each chapter in this section is devoted to a specific area for developing the whole child. Each of these chapters will contribute to the FIRM (Foundation, Inquiring Minds, Relationships, Mindset) framework.

You may even find that you have strengths in some of these areas of development. You may already have implemented some of the strategies that I will mention in this section. I found in my own classroom that I had some really great strategies I was using, but didn't even realize how valuable they were to the students' development. I also learned that through my years of teaching, some strategies were lost in the hustle to achieve academically. Later realizing the importance, I brought those strategies back to life in my classroom. I hope that you, too, will be able to identify your own strengths and hopefully learn the value of all that takes place in the busy day of an elementary classroom.

The purpose of this section is to help you understand which areas are important for developmental growth, why these areas are important, and how they affect the way a student learns. I will share practical strategies that you can easily implement in your classroom. I bet you already do some of what you will be reading about, but maybe you will gain a better understanding of how your students will benefit. I found that in my time teaching in inclusive classrooms, I was reminded that many of the strategies I was already using were in fact strengthening areas of developmental growth. It's always refreshing when you realize what you are doing is really making a difference. If you are anything like me, you love finding easy practical strategies that will make a big impact for your student's learning. Are you ready to slow down with me? Then let's go!

Teaching Resources marked with this thumbnail are included in the free *Slow Down! Children are Learning!* teacher resources pdf. Directions for downloading your FREE copy are in the front of the book.

Chapter 3

Executive Function Skills

"The increasingly competent executive functioning of children and adolescents enables them to plan and act in a way that makes them good students, classroom citizens, and friends."
— The Center on the Developing Child,
Harvard University

Have you ever been sitting in an IEP meeting, listening to your school psychologist explain to parents and teachers that their child has problems with executive function skills? Say what? Do you have a hard time wrapping your head around what that really means? Well, I did! And I have been known for being the teacher in the room who asks the questions that everyone else is thinking but doesn't ask. I know that I cannot fully make a difference for these kids if I can't wrap my own head around it! I also know that if I cannot wrap my head around what "executive function" means, then most likely the parents aren't quite sure either. So, I ask!

This term, executive function, is talked about more and more, because we know more about brain function than ever before. It is one of the most common phrases I hear during IEP meetings— "Executive Function Skills." Many students who have Individualized Education Plans (IEPs) experience delays in the development of their executive function skills. As I asked the questions and learned more about what this means, I realized that this is an area of brain development that needs to be continually worked on for all learners. For me, this was one of those things that I didn't learn about until I was well into my career. One of the many things that early childhood and elementary teachers are learning, as more and more is discovered about brain development, is that most students with learning disabilities have delays in executive function. We hear this all the time. However, what nobody is saying is that all of us need our executive function skills in order to achieve, not just the students who have it written into an IEP. I saw proof of this during my six years of teaching in inclusive kindergarten classrooms.

Luckily for me, our Speech and Language Pathologist (who was totally brilliant and had a passion for executive function) was teaching in my inclusive kindergarten classroom. There was one year in particular that most of the kindergarten students on speech IEPs were not on IEPs for speech sounds, but rather for executive function, which falls under the umbrella of communication. We tackled this issue through inclusion and what we found was that *every* student in the classroom of 25 kindergarteners (even those not on an IEP) grew tremendously in the area of executive function because we shifted our focus to meet those needs! This particular year was one that I will never forget. It was not just an aha! moment, but an aha! kind of year.

I wish that every regular education classroom teacher had the opportunity to teach the way that Kathy and I did that year. Our data proved that teaching in inclusive classrooms with IEP kids, in a class that had role models, is vital! It also proved the efficacy of developing executive function skills in the role models in our classroom, due to the extra opportunities for them to learn these skills and to lead others in their individual development. Our research also proved that working to develop these executive function skills is directly connected to student progress, achievement, independence, and self-confidence. Developing these skills proved to provide students with specific mental tools: impulse control, shifting attention, cognitive ability, and organization. These are the mental tools necessary to succeed with today's rigorous academics.

What Are Executive Function Skills?

Executive function skills are the skills that control how we initiate a task, adjust to problems, and negotiate obstacles, while organizing and prioritizing all of the steps and details. Phew! Isn't our brain amazing? When our executive function skills are working well, we can plan, focus, remember, multitask, and better control our thoughts and actions.

We can put executive function skills into three categories: Cognitive Flexible Attention, Working Memory, and Inhibitory Control.

Cognitive Flexible Attention

This is the ability to be flexible and shift our attention when necessary, whether this means focusing on a personal task, listening to the teacher speak, or participating in a lesson when your mind is somewhere else. Cognitive attention allows us to be present and to juggle many tasks. Picture the following scenario:

You are working on your lesson plans and deep in thought when a co-worker comes in to talk with you. You are listening to what they are saying. However, you continue to plug away with what you are planning for the week. You can hear your co-worker talking, but you are really thinking about what you are typing in your lesson plans. Then your co-worker asks, "Do you think that is what I should do?" Umm?!

You were so focused on typing your lesson plans that you were only half listening to what your co-worker was saying. You have no idea how to answer their question. Cognitive flexible attention allows you to stop typing, look at your co-worker and listen to them, have a conversation, then pick up where you left off in typing your lesson plans. This flexibility of attention is an executive function skill that wasn't used in this scenario. Luckily, we can develop this skill with the right strategies, practice, and effort.

Can you imagine being a child in a 1st grade classroom in today's schools? There is so much going on. Children must be able to shift their attention, or they miss out on important instruction. I believe that many students could even possibly be misdiagnosed with ADD/ADHD when in truth they are just lacking the development of executive function skills. If we intentionally taught elementary, middle school, and high school students strategies to develop their cognitive flexible attention maybe we would see more of our students at all grade levels with a better ability to focus and shift their attention when necessary.

Working Memory

This is how we store information. Our working memory allows us to remember important information. It manages the information, tasks, and things we learn. It allows us to process the information and access it when needed. Basically, the working memory is the "to-do list" in your mind that we continue to visit from time to time.

You have a very busy day ahead of you. You are getting out all of the materials needed for your day. Your students start to come into the classroom and get started with their morning routine as you go through your morning responsibilities. As you begin the first lesson of your day, the fire alarm goes off. Just then you remember that earlier in the week your principal told you to plan for a practice drill. You didn't remember, until you heard the alarm. The alarm triggered your memory. Technically you didn't forget about the practice drill, but because you didn't write it in your plans, it wasn't fresh in your mind. You were able to access the memory of your principal telling you to plan for it, right when you heard the alarm. This is working memory.

On a daily basis, we throw a lot of information at our students. Whether it is morning routines, rules and procedures, or responsibilities, our students have a lot to hold in their working memory. We can use strategies that will lessen the load for them. In this chapter you will learn strategies for supporting your students in processing information and accessing that information when necessary.

Inhibitory Control

This is the ability to control our actions and thoughts. It allows us to pause and think before we react, resist impulse, and keeps us on track. Inhibitory control helps us to know when to speak out and when to wait our turn. It is the skill that allows us to make good choices based on what we know to be acceptable. Most importantly, this skill helps us to be able to set goals and carry them out. Have you ever tried to work with somebody who lacked inhibitory control? I have!

This is a true story. A fellow teacher on your team storms into your classroom and starts to yell at you for something she heard that you said. Your students are just lining up for dismissal and standing right next to you at the door. This teacher continues to point at you and yell. (Seems extreme, I know, but this is true.) You remain calm and tell her that you will discuss this with her after dismissal. She storms out of your room shouting, "Nothing more needs to be discussed!"

Yikes! Right? This fellow teacher was lacking some inhibitory control. She was fired up and did not take the time to think through her actions. There are research-proven strategies that can be taught to both children and adults to develop inhibitory control. Oftentimes in schools, this job is given to the guidance counselor and/or behavior coaches. However, we can teach strategies for this throughout our daily interactions and experiences in our regular education classrooms.

Inhibitory control allows us to be good listeners, giving our brains optimal time to process what is going on around us. It prevents us from interrupting, allowing us to be good communicators. Having control over our inhibitions is something that comes with maturity. However, these skills can be developed at an early age when a child is provided with the proper lessons and strategies. Every child (actually, every adult, too) needs strategies for controlling their inhibitions. Think about the example of the teacher storming angrily into the classroom. If only somebody would have taught her at a young age to stop, think, and even count to 10, she could have much better expressed her concerns and handled herself in a much more professional manner.

Why Are Executive Function Skills Important for Learning?

Academic success strongly depends on a student's ability to plan, organize, prioritize tasks, shift attention, think flexibly, memorize content, and monitor their own progress. Executive function's role is to help students navigate what is required of them, beginning in preschool, and it increases as students progress through middle school and high school when they are expected to master more complex skills. As schoolwork gets harder and more complex, the lack of executive function skills will cause the student to feel overwhelmed and anxious and, as a result, it is quite possible they will fall behind. This often leads to exhaustion and a cycle of insecurities and even a low self-esteem.

Let's take a trip back to college. Sounds fun, right? Okay, so think about all the things you had to manage your first year of college—meals, keeping a clean dorm room, working a job to pay for your little car and insurance and cell phone, scheduling classes, getting to your classes, organizing your materials for your classes, studying, projects, professional groups, social groups, and of course time for your roommate and friends! And all the while there is no adult keeping you in line, no parent reminding you to do your homework. In fact, for the first time in your life you must act like an adult.

How did you handle it? Well, if you had strong executive function skills you probably made a to-do list, kept track of your responsibilities in a calendar or planner of some sort, stayed focused and on task, were able to prioritize, could shift your attention when necessary and get right back to what you initially had started, controlled your impulses to hang with friends when you had a project due, remembered to eat, and you even got enough rest so that you could make it to that early morning class on time the next day. Raise your hand if this was you!

I will be completely honest—that was not my experience. In fact, in my first year of college, I found myself more interested in the social part of school. I didn't realize how serious the course work actually would be. I had no idea how to study, until a friend of mine taught me some tricks she learned from a teacher in high school. It was difficult for me to choose to stay in and study if I knew there were friends getting together. I lacked inhibitory control. I lacked cognitive flexible attention. Thankfully, I was organized, determined, and confident enough to ask for help when needed. Boy, do I wish that I would have learned strategies that promoted the development of these types of skills when I was younger, giving me years to practice these strategies before I was expected to figure it out on my own.

Did you know that your brain is not fully developed until your mid-twenties? The frontal lobe (which controls executive function skills) is the last to fully develop. So, for this reason alone, I'm guessing you probably didn't master all the details of your college life either! Can you see why teens and young adults are so stressed?

Can you start to understand why so many kids have such high anxiety rates? The part of their brain that allows them to handle it all isn't even fully developed yet. They cannot function to the highest ability of the expectations given to them.

Can we help them? Yes, we can! We need to be intentionally developing these skills in our students throughout their academic career, starting in kindergarten and continuing on throughout their grade school years. When our students have developed executive function skills, they will be more likely to be prepared to handle their academic progress before they go off to college, where they are expected to manage it all on their own. The key is just that—we need to start teaching these strategies early, helping them out far before we expect them to independently juggle everything and find success.

Executive function skills begin developing in the first five years of a child's life. During this time, the best way to develop these skills is by providing children with a nurturing childhood—free play, guided play, allowing them to be curious, and allowing them to solve problems are all part of a nurturing childhood. This means letting them explore and figure things out. This means holding them when they are upset and showing them that they can calm down and control how they are feeling. This also means providing them with the proper tools and strategies that will set them up for lifelong success. Before the age of five, we can begin to develop this part of their brain by providing opportunities for discovery, while we nurture and support them. Isn't it interesting that age five is when we recommend kids start kindergarten?

Elementary school is the optimal time to focus on developing executive function skills. These skills will build a foundation for academic success. We cannot expect children entering school to be able to handle academic rigor without the proper developmental skills for managing their learning. For this reason, we must focus on teaching and developing executive function skills in our regular elementary classrooms in order to enable all of our students to achieve success.

How to Develop Executive Function Skills in Your Classroom

We know that executive function skills take time to develop. In fact, the frontal lobe is the last part of our brain to develop. Executive function skills begin to develop at birth. However, they are not fully developed until our mid-twenties. This fact alone proves that we must allow ourselves to focus on developing executive function skills over time, through the early years of learning, as well as into middle school and high school. Executive function skills are not just something we can teach and move on. These skills are not as cut and dried as some of the other skills that we teach our students. No, these brain functions are developed through time.

Think of all that goes into a garden. You prepare the soil, plant the seeds, water, wait, and wait some more. You pray for sunshine, water some more, and wait. You weed the garden, provide supports for some of the plants, and oftentimes you have to figure out how you will debug the plants that are starting to grow. At harvest time, you get to sit back and enjoy what you took time to create!

Just like a garden, executive function skills will take time and the right steps to properly develop. In this chapter, you will learn simple ways to use each of the following ingredients to develop executive function skills in your students:

- Time
- Teaching Strategies
- Classroom Procedures
- Lessons to Teach
- Tools for Your Classroom

Time

Executive function skills take time. As we've already learned they can take up to 20 years to develop. The early learning years are the prime time to work on this part of the brain. Unlike many of our grade level teaching standards, we cannot just teach these skills and move on. Executive function skills are developed through purposeful strategies that are repeated year after year. When students come to kindergarten, they have to be taught how to function in school. This means lots of planning, organizing, remembering processes and procedures, accessing new and old information, and so much more. We must start slow as we show them each and every step—for example, teaching students to get in a line. (Pause for laughter!) If you've ever seen the video of the little girl rounding up kittens, you will be laughing with me right now because that is exactly what teaching kindergarteners to line up is like.

But we do have to take the time to teach them. Each year, they will get better at lining up. However, you will need to give them new instructions each year. The strategies that develop executive function skills will need to be revisited and added onto as the students progress in school. Just like our garden, we have to continue to water, give sun, and pull the weeds as the time goes on.

Kindergarten is where we prepare the soil and plant the seeds. This is

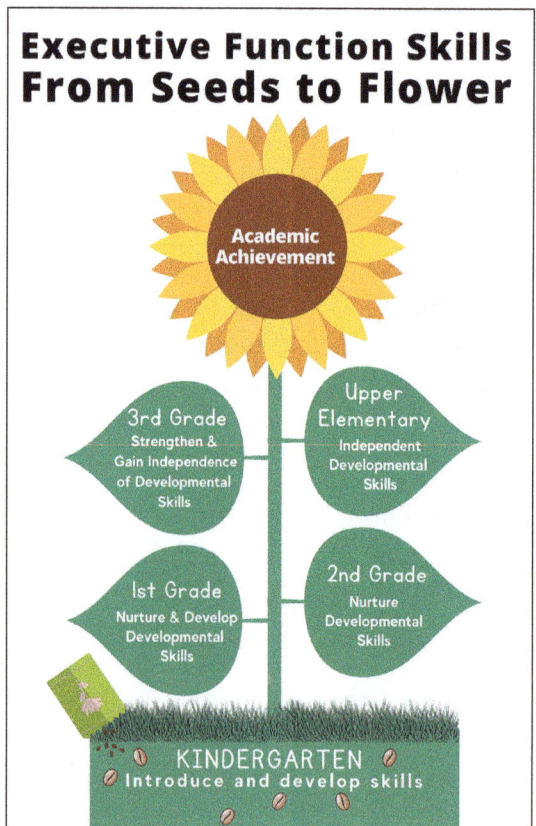

Executive Function Skills From Seeds to Flower

Academic Achievement

3rd Grade — Strengthen & Gain Independence of Developmental Skills

Upper Elementary — Independent Developmental Skills

1st Grade — Nurture & Develop Developmental Skills

2nd Grade — Nurture Developmental Skills

KINDERGARTEN — Introduce and develop skills

when new strategies are taught through modeling and monitoring. Kids at this age are not able to manage time and space, pre-plan, organize ideas, and/or visualize an end result. They need to be walked through the process step by step. They need to be provided with visuals and time trackers. They need tasks broken into smaller tasks. They need to be given the tools to self-advocate, use social cues, and allow for time to process information.

After we plant the seeds in kindergarten, we water our garden and watch it grow and develop. This happens throughout our primary grades, grades K-3. We water our garden when we practice using these strategies until they become habitual routines.

These executive function skills should start to become habitual routines by 3rd or 4th grade. You see, when we learn something and then move on, expecting that students will naturally mature the skill, we are sadly mistaken. But when we continue to revisit the strategies they know and build upon them, our students will become more independent and confident about being in control of their learning. We are essentially training their brain to create good habits. When the habits are formed, they are able to effortlessly juggle rigorous academics. Let me explain—

A friend of mine has this routine that she does every evening. Each night when she is getting ready for bed, she picks out two outfits, checks her color-coded calendar, and makes a to-do list for the next day. I asked her once how she got into the habit of doing this. Her response was, "I don't know. It's something I've always done."

As we talked about this routine of hers, she explained that when she was a kid, her mom would always lay out two outfits for her, one that was comfy and one that was cute or fashionable. This way, in the morning she didn't have to spend a lot of time deciding. She said that her mom had always kept a daily to-do list for herself and, as she got older, she just started to do the same. The tip for color coding her calendar came from a middle school teacher she once had. She learned that if she gave each different activity a color, then she could easily see how her time was being spent. This helped her to make her daily to-do list and to get everything done effectively and efficiently.

You see, my friend didn't just wake up one day and begin to meticulously manage her day. This routine was a habit she formed at a very young age. Her mother may not have realized that when she was picking out school clothes each night, she was actually developing her daughter's executive function skills! Her mother also may not have realized that making her own nightly to-do list was a way to model how to manage tasks and time for her daughter. The middle school teacher who gave her students the tip to color code their calendars may or may not have done that intentionally to develop executive functions skills, but it worked! Many years—in fact, a decade of practicing—created a habit that will forever assist my friend in living a successful life.

This is how good habits are formed. We establish a routine that is successful and practice that same routine until it becomes a habit. Eventually we can do it without even thinking about it. Until a habit is formed, we must be intentional about developing executive function skills in this same way. That is what we want—to train our students to have good habits that will make navigating their life (school, work, play, achievements) easier!

Teaching Strategies

A strategy is a way of doing something. The way we teach will determine the development of our students. There are many different strategies for teaching, and determining which strategy to use depends on the skill that needs to be developed. When being intentional about developing executive function skills we have already established that we must take our time.

I would like to share with you two teaching strategies that will help develop executive function skills when used across your curriculum. You may be teaching a lesson in writing, reading, or math with an academic standard in mind, or you may be teaching your students a classroom procedure or how to use a learning tool. Either way, you can accomplish your goal by using a teaching strategy that is working the frontal lobe and developing those executive function skills. So even though we teachers always feel like there isn't enough time, we don't have to add anything to give our executive function skills a workout! These two strategies can be used to teach any skill while simultaneously developing executive function skills.

The 3 Ms: Model, Monitor, and Measure

This strategy is successful across the curriculum for teaching students. It works because consistency creates good habits. I'm sure that many of you already teach in this way, but maybe you just haven't put a name on it. This is true for me as well! I very naturally fall into the pattern of this teaching strategy without even thinking about it. Even though you also probably teach in this way, you may not realize how much it really is benefiting your students' brain development. This pattern is a cycle that repeats itself as the learner makes progress.

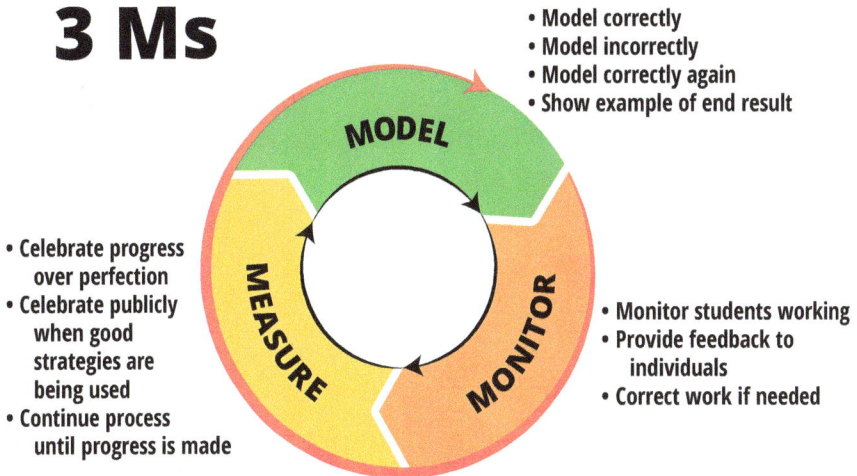

3 Ms

MODEL
- Model correctly
- Model incorrectly
- Model correctly again
- Show example of end result

MONITOR
- Monitor students working
- Provide feedback to individuals
- Correct work if needed

MEASURE
- Celebrate progress over perfection
- Celebrate publicly when good strategies are being used
- Continue process until progress is made

Model

We teach our students, regardless of their grade, the specific strategies and show them exactly how to use the strategy through modeling. Show them! Use role play to show them exactly how to do whatever it is that you are teaching. An important part of modeling is to provide your students with a visual image of what the end result should look like. Remember, young students are not able to create a mental image of the finished product. You have to show them. Once they have seen the end goal, and watched the process modeled, you can then have some fun and model it the wrong way to see if they catch the mistake. Students love that! Anything to make it memorable.

Monitor

After we physically show them how, we need to observe them using the strategy. This means offering feedback, correcting and encouraging them, and continuing to monitor. This can take some patience and oftentimes will send us back to modeling again. We can also make observations and use our findings to plan strategically in our classrooms. A good example of this is setting up our classroom seating based on our observations of student ability. Students with weaker executive function skills will benefit tremendously from sitting next to a student who would act as a good model for them. When we see somebody else doing something the right way, it makes us reflect and reconsider how we are doing it. Models or mentors play an important role in learning and succeeding.

Measure

When you see your students using their executive function skills and the specific strategies that you've taught, point it out to them. These skills are often taken for granted or not noticed at all. Say things like, "Wow, I love how you decided to make a to-do list of your own, so that you could get everything done!" This will remind them that using these strategies really does help them get the job done well. You can even celebrate a student with the whole class!

Now that we know we need to teach strategies to develop executive function skills using the 3 Ms method (Model, Monitor, and Measure), we need to know what strategies will actually mature and develop executive function skills.

Plan-Tran-Execute

Plan-Tran-Execute is a strategy for transitioning from one thing to another. Oh, how I love transitions! A transition can make or break your class. If you give these kids too much time in between one thing and another, you will lose them. If you do not show them exactly how to transition, they will take your transition and make it their own personal social hour and fun time. Another pitfall of transitions is forgetfulness and distractions. This is not because your students are not paying attention; it's because their executive function skills are not yet developed. You have to plan ahead in order to prevent these pitfalls from happening to you and your students.

Plan-Tran-Execute is a strategy that will help students pre-plan what they are about to do, visualize it, repeat it, and execute it without being distracted. Pre-planning is very difficult for young children and even for a lot of adults. In the early elementary years, due to the lack of executive function skills, a student is mentally unable to picture the end result until they've actually walked through the process. You see, once you've given them instructions and sent them to get the job done, a lot happens between the pre-planning and execution. There are many distractions that can prevent someone from ever executing what they had planned.

Have you ever made a "to-do list" and then when you actually got started with your day, you changed it or didn't even pay attention to it because something distracted you? I think we've all experienced that. Have you ever set out to get something in your house, and you've been on your way to get it, but then you were distracted and never did end up going to find what you were originally looking for? Have you ever told your child to go to their room and get their dirty clothes and they come back to you and say, "What was I supposed to get?" or not even return at all because they ended up seeing a book they love and decided to read it. This is why you need to learn to use the strategy of plan-tran-execute! This strategy will help bridge the gap between pre-planning and execution of the task at hand.

Picture your own classroom. Let's say you tell your students that they are going to get out their silent reading books and find a comfy spot to read. Then you transition and many students do not follow your directions. You take a closer look and notice that one student stopped to blow their nose and noticed a candy wrapper in the trash and his brain ventured off to think about where it came from and how he could get some candy. Another student noticed that her friend didn't hear your instructions so she stopped to help her friend out and they started discussing where they would sit at lunch and who they would play with at recess. All the while, other students were also distracted by something that occurred between the pre-planning (your instructions) and execution (getting the books out and finding their comfy reading spot).

Does that description sound familiar? Well, it wasn't actually that they weren't listening to you or that they did not want to follow your directions. They weren't being defiant. They just got side-tracked. You see, a lot happens between the planning phase and the execution phase. So how do we bridge that gap of time where the distractions are taking place?

"Plan-Tran-Execute" is a strategy for giving the instructions, transitioning, and executing that will help students to focus on the task and be less likely to get side-tracked or forget. The first time you use this strategy you will have to teach them how it works. Students need to understand why they are taking the time to do this. You are giving that brain muscle a workout to strengthen the part of the brain that will help them plan, transition, or move from one thing to the next, and get the task done without allowing all that other stuff distract them! This will look different in each grade level, but no matter how old they are, you can still follow these simple steps:

Planning for the Transition

Instruct/Repeat

The first step of the planning part of this strategy is to give your instructions and have your students repeat them aloud, basically like a call and response, only it's instruct and repeat! For instance:

Teacher: "Okay, boys and girls, you are going to clean off your desk, turn in your paper, and get your silent reading book out. Repeat after me: clean desk, turn in paper, silent reading."

Visualize the Task

The next step of the planning is to help your students visualize what they will be doing or picture how it will look. Go over the instructions again and have the students look to where they are going to do each step of the directions. They can even point to the place where each step will happen. You might say the following:

- *Clean Desk*—There will be nothing on your desk. Think about where you will put everything that you have out right now. Don't do it yet, just think about the actions you will have to take in order to get the desk cleaned off.
- *Turn in Paper*—Everyone show me where you will go to turn in your paper. (Students all point.) Right! So, you will take your paper over to the tray. When we repeat "turn in paper," we can point to the paper turn-in tray.
- *Silent Reading*—Everyone show me where you will find your silent reading materials. Point there. So, when we repeat the instruction "silent reading," you will point to where you get those materials.

Repeat and Point

The last step of the planning part of this strategy is to repeat and make a motion. You repeat each step as a class while pointing to the location or making some sort of motion for remembering the action.

- Teacher: Clean off desk.
- Students: Clean off desk (point to desk).
- Teacher: Turn in paper.
- Students: Turn in paper (point to turn-in tray).
- Teacher: Silent reading.
- Students: Silent reading (point to silent reading materials).

Execute the Transition

This is the action part of the process. When you are confident that your students know what their job is, you send them off to do it. I like to send them off using this call and response strategy: Instead of counting, "One, two, three, go—" I say, "Plan, Tran—" and students usually shout, "Execute!"

And off they go—hopefully without getting distracted! Of course, this doesn't remove the distractions. However, the repetition and motions will make their working memory stronger than the distractions that may cross their paths. If they are distracted, their working memory will be easily accessed because of the Plan-Tran-Execute strategy that you have taught to them and used time and time again.

Lessons That Develop Executive Function Skills

There are certain things that elementary teachers have to teach, such as how to line up, that other teachers may not realize. We take time to teach these things because it helps our students in the long run. These lessons are necessary to teach in order for a child to thrive in school, yet are not technically part of the state standards. These are lessons that teach students how to function, relate to others, communicate, and advocate for their own learning.

Often times teachers will just assume that kids will learn these things along the way. But we couldn't be more wrong. Sure, some will figure things out, because each student has unique strengths and weaknesses. However, if we assume that our students will just figure it out, there will be many who slip through the cracks or will be affected when learning gets more difficult. If we revisit my philosophy of building a F.I.R.M. foundation for learning, we will start to see a direct connection between executive function skills and building that F.I.R.M. foundation. I will share a variety of lessons/mini-lessons that do not take too much time, but are necessary for developing executive function skills in our students. These lessons/mini-lessons will teach students how to do the following:

- Self-Advocate
- Communicate (Listening and Speaking)
- Plan and Organize
- Collaborate (Team Work)
- Regulate Emotions

Self-Advocating Mini-Lessons

Teaching students when and how to advocate for themselves is vital. They need to know that it is okay to ask questions. Kids need to be taught strategies for doing so, especially in the early elementary years. My brilliant Speech/Language Pathologist friend, Kathy, taught my class the following self-advocating mini-lessons that teach students how to help their brain understand what to do if they are not quite sure of what is expected. I observed the benefits that each student in my class gained from these lessons. I continued to teach these mini-lessons after my years with Kathy teaching in inclusive classrooms. Remember to use the 3 Ms (Model, Monitor, Measure) when you teach the following lessons.

Please Repeat

Teach your class to ask you to repeat the instructions if they missed part of your instruction. If they didn't hear you or got distracted, it's okay. It happens to all of us. Teach them to raise their hand and say, "Could you please repeat?" Use a motion for memory when you teach this. For instance, hold your two hands in the "thumbs up" position and rotate your arms in a circle to show a repeat-like motion, all while saying "please repeat." You can also use this when you can't hear or can't understand a student! Modeling the use of a strategy is a great way to keep it consistent and show that we all need to self-advocate. It may feel silly to teach this, but it will show them the importance of asking for help. It will let those students who aren't quite sure know that it is okay—actually expected!—to ask for help. We want our students to feel confident in asking for help.

Please Explain

This is the same concept as above, but students ask the teacher to explain rather than repeat. This should be used when a student knows what you said but needs it explained in a different way. Applaud them publicly when they self-advocate. This will show others that it is a good thing to do.

Using Clues From Peers

Sometimes students just lose track of what they are doing. We can teach our students to use clues from around the room to solve this problem. Practice using clues by giving your students a scenario and have them consider where they could look for the answer. They can refer to anchor charts in the class or observations of what their peers are doing. You could ask them, "What if you are not sure how to spell a word? Where are there clues in the room that could help you?" Then your students can point to your word wall or the charts that are visible to them.

Another important type of clue in the classroom is within their peers. You might say to your students, "If you get distracted and aren't sure what you are supposed to be doing, what clue could help you?" The other students! Believe it or not, in early elementary grades, they need to be taught to look around and see what others are doing. Because they do not have the executive function skills needed and often lack self-confidence, they are not able to look at a classroom situation and picture how they fit into it. Teaching your students to use their classmates as models for what to do is a great strategy. It's one that we just assume kids will catch on to, but this is not always so. Taking the time to teach them how to use their clues around the room will ensure that they are capable of this self-advocating method.

Listening/Communicating Mini-Lessons

I use "listening" to mean "attending to what another person communicates." Before beginning any of these mini-lessons, take stock of your students' communication abilities. If you have a student who has a hearing aid, be sure to work with their SLP to make sure it's set up correctly. If you have a student who is supported by a sign language interpreter, work with their special education teacher to confirm they can participate in all of your lessons. Don't assume all of your students use their ears to listen!

Being a good listener is something that we can teach our students. So, yes, you have to teach your students how to be a good listener! Each student in your class has a variability that needs to be acknowledged. There are many different factors to consider: ability to hear, sensitivity to sound and movement, ability to focus, just to name a few. Also, we need to think about how hearing and listening are different. There are many things to consider when teaching your students how to be good listeners.

Executive function plays a big role in being a good listener. Your brain must be able to hear what the person is saying, understand it, organize the thoughts, make connections, and control your impulse to interject or become distracted. Executive function skills allow you to focus attention and know when to shift your attention. Lessons that teach and practice good listening skills need to be conducted in every grade level. The more your students are intentional about being good listeners, the more likely this will become a habit that provides lasting advantages throughout their lives.

Our job is to teach them some practical things that good listeners do. So, what do good listeners do? Think about how you know when your students are listening to you. What do they do? How are they positioned? What do their faces look like when they are listening? You and I both know that when our class is not really listening, there is a different feeling in the classroom. If you have ever felt this, you will also know how it feels when your students are actively listening to you. Think about it. Ask your students the same question. How do you know when others around you are listening?

I have listed a couple of must-do mini-lessons and daily activities that promote being a good listener. As you read through these lessons you may be thinking, "Duh, I already do this." Well, then let it be a pat on the back that you are heading in the right direction for supporting growth of executive function skills! But you may also be thinking, "Seriously, my students shouldn't need such a basic lesson; they should already know this." The truth, though, is that many students do not just automatically do these simple things which will help them develop skills that will promote a successful learning experience. There are simple lessons that should only take 10-15 minutes to teach, along with continued modeling of the strategy, and reminders that will eventually create good habits.

The following are must-do mini-lessons and guidelines for good listening and communicating:

Good Listening Position

Sounds funny, but it's true. If you are not currently teaching your class what it looks like to be a good listener, start NOW! Lucy (our fictional student) is a good listener. She chooses to listen with her whole body and with purpose. One of the ways we can show respect to someone communicating with us is by giving them our full attention. Students are so used to multi-tasking that we have to model for them what it looks like to make listening the only thing they do. I call it "one-way listening." One-way listening is when a student can hear your voice, but may or may not comprehend what you said enough to actually do something with it. The reason it's "one way" is because the listener has no clue if they understood what the speaker is communicating. I know that there have been times when you have been giving instructions while your students are putting things away, moving around the room, or are even on their computers or other form of technology. They may hear you, but they are not being good listeners. Showing the speaker that you can stop, look, and listen is a form of respect that they will need in order to live a successful life.

Lucy Listener has attentive eyes and listening ears. She sits facing the speaker and keeps her hands in her lap. Too many of us think we can be a good listener while moving around or participating in other actions but it's a lot harder than we think. Lucy helps you teach your students to be aware of how their body is positioned when they are able to hear, understand, wonder, and respond to what is being said. Teach them that when they are able to do those things, their brain is better able to focus, grow, and learn.

They will need to practice this because it does not come naturally to young kids. Even in the upper elementary grades this should be taught, modeled, and practiced. Lucy is a great model for being an active listener. After you model how Lucy listens, you should have them practice so that they can form the habit of being an attentive listener.

Of course The 3 Ms (Model, Monitor, and Measure) are in place here just as they are with most lessons that you teach. This is not only important while in your class for the purpose of knowing what to do. It is a life skill.

Lucy Follows the 5 Ls for Listening:

1. Look with your eyes.
2. Listen with your ears.
3. Locked lips.
4. Legs crisscross.
5. Hands in your Lap.

I know that this seems a bit "old school" and don't worry. I'm not suggesting that anyone get their hand cracked with a ruler or have to stand in the corner because they did not follow Lucy's 5 Listening Tips. However, the younger your students are, the more structure they need while listening. Their brain is easily distracted and has not yet developed inhibitory control. So teaching them this type of body positioning will, in fact, help them to develop focused attention and inhibitory control. The older your students are the better they get at focusing on their own and being able to shift their attention.

I Can Listen to Grow My Brain

Teach students to stop what they are doing and turn their body to face the speaker. This lesson helps students understand the brain's role in listening and understanding. It helps students to realize that their brain is a muscle that grows when they learn. Teaching this lesson will help elementary students see the difference between simply hearing and listening for understanding. A printable book illustrating whole-body listening is included in the free resource packet mentioned in the front of this book. This lesson and resource is a great follow up to Lucy Listener.

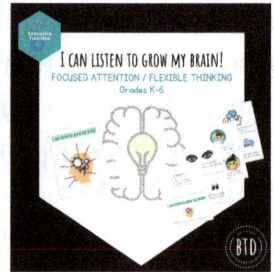

Attentive Eyes, Listening Ears

My students hear me say this over and over: "Attentive eyes, listening ears." It has even become a call and response to get their attention. One day, after many days of hearing me say this, I said, "Attentive eyes" and the class got quiet and then finished it themselves by saying, "listening ears." I love it! Teaching your students that our eyes help us to listen is a mini-lesson (more of a conversation) that they easily understand. Even though our ears do the work of hearing, when we use our eyes to look at the speaker, it not only shows respect, but it helps our brain to focus and understand what is being said.

I know that making eye contact is not easy for all kids. In fact, many students with disabilities or those who come from different cultures and races may feel some tension with making eye contact. Be considerate of those who struggle with this. We should never punish those who choose not to make eye contact. If a child is able to listen for understanding without making eye contact, that's fine. We should always consider the class make-up. Also consider the larger goal at hand. You are teaching your students how to best understand what they hear.

Michele Borba, the author of *UnSelfie*, writes that making eye contact can, in fact, help create empathy. In other words, it can help us connect to what is being said and help us to have an understanding of how the speaker feels. She even offers tips such as focusing on the color of the speaker's eyes or having a staring contest with those who feel tension in making eye contact. The root of tuning in and making a brain impact is not only hearing but understanding. Making eye contact will help with this. Show them and practice with them what good eye contact feels like. You might even mention that sometimes a good listener will nod or smile or make different expressions to show they are listening to what is being said.

Interrupting Chicken

There is a wonderful children's book called *Interrupting Chicken* by David Ezra Stein. This is a fun way to show young kids what happens when we constantly interrupt. Because of the lack of executive function skills, young students vary in ability to control inhibitions. They get so excited about what they are hearing that they just blurt out what is on their minds. They may show that they are making connections, which in fact means they are actively listening. However, learning to hold their thought and retrieve it at the right time will also assist in the development of their working memory, which is also an executive function skill. This will get better as the executive function skills continue to develop.

In regard to interrupting, there is a very interesting concept called Cooperative Overlapping. This is the idea that conversation will overlap due to the conversationalists being enthusiastic about the topic at hand. A form of this is often used by classroom teachers to see if their students are in fact listening to what is being said. For example, a teacher may be telling a story and then lead her students to finish her sentence, thus proving that they are listening and comprehending. Sociolinguist Deborah Tannen calls Cooperative Overlapping a form of active listening, which she says is more acceptable in some cultures than in others. However, when we are working with the development of the executive function skills, the more we practice becoming active listeners—practicing shifting our focus from one speaker to another, and accessing information from our working memory—the more we will continue to develop these vital skills.

I would recommend teaching this lesson to middle school and high school students. Now more than ever, people think it is acceptable to multitask while listening to somebody speak. Making eye contact with the speaker is something that I feel is being lost as we dive deeper into the digital world. Expect your students to listen with their whole body. They will benefit from it in the end, for sure!

News Flash

This is a daily practice that the kids love! News Flash teaches your students to listen well enough to report out. News Flash works great at the beginning of your day. You simply take 5-10 minutes for a couple of your students to share a "News Flash." This can be anything that is on their mind that they want to share with the class. I like to give a microphone to the speaker. The first speaker might say, "We went out for ice cream last night!" and then they will hand off the microphone to somebody else. The next person will say, "Johnny went out for ice cream last night! I am going to visit my grandma today after school." Then they pass the microphone and it continues. Just before the microphone is passed for the last time, the student passing it will say, "Emily will be our last News Flash for today."

After Emily is done sharing, she can call on three friends to ask her questions about the topic she shared. The students asking the questions may need to be reminded that they must ask a question, not share a connection or another New Flash. News Flash teaches the students to focus enough to listen and understand, shift their attention, change positions to face the speaker, and control their impulses to interrupt. It takes no more than 10 minutes, and it develops skills that are so important! News Flash works for every grade level. Let's face it, who doesn't like to share?

Listen and Design

For this activity, you simply describe something that you are visualizing in your mind. As you describe it, you ask the students to try to picture it in their minds too. Then you give them time to draw what you described and share it with the class. They love this! These lessons are great for days when you know you will be having a substitute teacher, or if you just have extra time to fill.

Mind Movies

Teach the kids to create a movie in their mind as you read to the class. This may be more difficult for some than others. You may even need to explain what this means. Have the students think about the main character. You may review the facts—for instance, a tall cat wearing a hat comes to the house when the parents are gone—then ask the students if they are able to picture that in their mind. You can even have the students draw what they are able to remember about the main character or the problem in the story. It's interesting to see how different each student's mind movie is. The really great part is there is no right way. Practicing this gives your brain a workout for working memory.

This is a really fun way to teach homophones too. You give them a homophone verbally (not in a sentence, just the word), for instance "see/sea." You tell them to form a mind movie using the homophone "see/sea." Then you have them draw and label their picture. When they show their quick sketch to the class you can discuss the difference between "see/sea." This helps their brain to focus and remember in order to complete a task.

Students love making mind movies! Whether or not a student is actually able to have a vision in their mind, we know that their working memory is developing because they can access the information that was received by the brain. What other areas of your curriculum could you use this? Being able to access their working memory will help them throughout their education and can be practiced across the content areas.

Planning and Organizing Mini-Lessons

Raise your hand if you've ever witnessed a teacher dump a student's desk out on the floor. Ugh! I cringe just thinking about it! I hope you were never that kid—or that teacher. These kids are *not* being bad or lazy. All this does is shame them for having underdeveloped organization skills. Many kids develop these skills naturally, while others need to be taught how. The expectations need to be taught through the 3Ms (Model, Monitor, Measure).

Organizing Supplies

Show your students exactly how their supplies should be organized. You may even have to do it for some students. Every supply has a home. This also goes for lockers and desks. Some kids will need you to do it for them and monitor it consistently. You can also take a picture of their organized materials and give it to them to keep as a reminder of where everything goes. This can be very helpful in centers or in community supplies.

I like to hang a picture of the math manipulatives and how they should look if they are properly put away. You can measure students' success by doing consistent quick checks. At the end of each week, take time to reorganize materials so that you can start the next week organized and ready to learn. Celebrate when you find students who are successfully keeping their materials organized. As you work with your students and hold them accountable to your expectations, they will strengthen and continue to develop the skills necessary for organizing.

Desk Fairy

This is just a simple and fun way to motivate your students to keep their materials organized. I'd love to say this is a great way to develop the skill of being organized but it actually is just a simple tool for accountability and a way to form consistency with the hopes of creating great habits. First, I must start by saying that we cannot expect all kids to be able to do this naturally. Remember the kid who had his desk dumped in front of the teacher? We never want to jeopardize our students' mental or emotional state because we expect them to have skills that are not yet developed. This is where we have to be intentional about having a weekly or bi-weekly desk check. You simply give the students a designated time that everyone does a desk check and gets their materials organized. Then on random occasions, the desk fairy visits and leaves behind cards with a reward of some sort saying they loved how organized the students were. You can do this as a whole group reward or leave a note for individuals. This even works in upper elementary. Even though

they are older, they will still play along when there is something positive that comes along with it.

Directed Drawings

Directed drawings are one strategy that requires attentive listening, focus, and the ability to follow step-by-step instructions. Directed drawings give a student's brain a workout they can handle. During a directed drawing, there is step-by-step modeling from the teacher. You monitor each step as they work, and they must stay on task to keep up with the directions. Then creativity is offered in the end when they paint, color, or design their drawing. Don't leave directed drawings for art class! They help to develop executive function skills and are also a fun way to celebrate the seasons or holidays. In my class we did a directed drawing for each month or holiday.

Step-by-Step Crafts

Letter crafts or other simple crafts are a quick 10-minute activity that students love! In kindergarten we used each letter of the alphabet. In other grades you can choose any skill: shapes, fractions, nouns, and so on. You simply provide the small pieces, give step-by-step directions (verbally or written), and give your students 10 minutes to complete the task. Following step-by-step instructions helps to develop executive function skills of planning and organizing. Planning and organizing take place physically and mentally. We can provide opportunities for our students to plan and organize both their thoughts and their physical surroundings. Asking a student to place an object on the top right corner of a space will tell you a lot about how their brain plans and organizes. For this reason, doing simple step-by-step crafts will allow them to work this part of their brain.

Depending on the grade level, you can do these types of activities as teacher-directed or allow students to follow directions independently. It just breaks my heart when I hear teachers say there is no time for crafts or that their grade level is too old for little crafts.

All kids like to be creative and do crafts. They are fun and they work a system of the brain that needs to be developed.

Webs

Webs are used to organize thoughts. I'm sure many of you already use webs in many different ways. But have you realized that those webs actually work to teach your student's brain how to organize the information that is being learned? How often do you revisit the webs that you create in your classroom? I know that we all typically hang them in our room for our students to refer to, but do you walk your students through the steps of actually using the web? Revisiting your web of ideas and taking it a step further will also assist in the development of the executive function skills.

The information that was brainstormed, organized on a web, then used to produce something requires your students to use their frontal lobe in so many ways. They have to wonder, connect, share, organize thoughts, then come back later to access information that was tucked away in their working memory. Flexible cognitive attention and working memory get a great workout when you use your webs with intention!

Categorizing

Putting items into categories is also a great way to develop the executive function skills. We do this to identify shapes, learn word families, make connections, and make inferences. We have to access prior knowledge and use new observations, which is a great workout for our brain. One of my very favorite ways to practice this is with candy! That's right, nothing motivates a student quite like candy. Every year, no matter the grade, I do a fun activity with all my leftover Halloween candy. I also buy some full size bars to put in the mix.

The students sit around the rug in a circle and they know immediately what I have because I put it in my Halloween bucket. Before I spill the candy out onto the floor, I tell them that they will get to have a piece at the end of the lesson, but they are not allowed to touch the candy until they are given permission. This is when your students will have to practice controlling their inhibitions! Only the teacher gets to touch the candy.

First, I model how the game works by telling them that they will guess the candy I am describing but I do not want them to shout it out. They must control their natural tendency to shout out the answer. They are to raise their hand when they think they know it. I start to give them attributes of the candy such as: "It is in an orange wrapper." "The package has many candies in it." "It is shaped like a rectangle." When many of the students think they know the answer, I then go through the attributes again and separate the candies into categories and we name the categories: orange package, rectangle, many candies, and so on. By now, the whole class should know and be excited to answer.

Naming attributes, grouping them, and naming the category will give your students executive function skills a workout! You can also work on literacy skills in with this game, by using categories such as: beginning sounds, number of syllables, and rhymes with—. Depending on the grade you teach, you can change this game up lots of different ways.

KWL Charts

The good old KWL has been used for decades. The question is: did you know the reason for using it? Yes, of course we want to ignite that prior knowledge. Well, I will be the first to admit, that I didn't always understand just how important that is. I knew that it helped with making connections and keeping their interest in the topic, but what I didn't know is that asking your students "What do you already know about it?" is actually activating the frontal lobe and putting their executive function skills to work.

Again, giving these skills a workout is the only way to develop and mature them. When a student considers what they already know, they are accessing information from past experiences and using the working memory. This step is so important in the learning process.

Next, when using a KWL, we ask the students what they want to know. This step sparks an interest. It allows them to become an active participant. It also gives them a drive to seek out information. I've got news for you! Letting your students explore what is meaningful to them will make a world of difference when it comes to engagement. For this reason alone, help them get their questions answered, even if it strays from your plan or standard that is given to you.

The last step is going back and documenting what they learned. So often this step is skipped. I would be willing to bet you've left many KWL charts without completing this step, because you ran out of time and you needed to move on. Am I right? I know I'm right because I'm guilty of it! Listen, we think that it's no big deal, the test is over, they did the learning, right? Well, this last step is when the students can go back and access all of this new information that they have learned. This final step will develop the executive function skills by revisiting the process used to learn the skill at hand. It will allow your brain to check off the list, if you will.

I get that we are in a hurry and maybe your other teammates have moved on, but you have to be willing to slow down and finish the process so that your students will develop the skills that are vital to managing their learning. Taking the time to develop the executive function skills will give a student's brain the tools needed for learning along the way. Yes, we've all used these charts, but did you know how beneficial they actually are?

Checklists

Checklists help students to stay on task and track their own progress. It helps their brain to focus, and to shift focus as they move through their own list. There are several ways to use checklists in class:

- *Individualized Lists*—There are times that you will need to make different lists for different students. There are even times when you have a certain student who will always need a checklist on their desk. You can laminate a checklist and use a wipe-off marker so that you aren't using a new paper each time a list is required.
- *Whole Class Checklist*—When students are working on several different things, you can write a simple checklist on the board. The student simply works through the list. It is beneficial to make the list in the order of the priority to get things done.
- *Center Checklists*—Keeping a checklist at each center will help keep your students focused on the task at hand. It could be a list of pictures or written tasks that need to be completed at each center. If you allow your students to do free choice centers, you may also use a checklist to help them remember which centers they have already visited.

You must know your students and understand their developmental needs before making a checklist. If they are a kindergarten student with weak executive function skills, you may just give them one task at a time. The more developed their executive function skills are, the more items they can handle on a checklist.

A checklist alone is not a tool that will strengthen executive function skills. However, the process for creating the list and using it will. Let me explain. We previously discussed how young learners or learners with underdeveloped executive function skills are not capable of picturing an end result. So, for example, you show a student what the result looks like (e.g., an actual picture of the end result), then work backward with the student in order to create the steps needed to get those results. This is when the executive function skills get used. They now have ownership of planning out the steps necessary for completing the task. This becomes the checklist. You must involve the student in creating and planning the list in order for it to make a difference.

Emotional Regulation Mini-Lessons

Inhibitory control is the ability to gain control over what feels like a natural instinct. Think of when a young child gets frustrated. What is the first thing they do? They cry! What about when they see their mom after a long day at work? They get up and run as fast as they can into their mother's arms shouting, "Mommy, mommy!" Now think about those same scenarios but with a teenager. What does a teenager do when they feel frustrated? They definitely don't cry—at least not in front of people! You see, maturity and experience has told them that crying over certain things is not acceptable at their age. What about when they see their mom after a long day at school? I mean, most teens ask their parents to drop them off down the road! They don't even want to be seen with their parents. This doesn't mean they didn't want to run to their parent for a hug. It just goes to show that at this age, they are able to choose to control their natural inhibitions.

Controlling your natural inhibitions is something we all have to learn how to do in order to be a team player, good communicator, and a respectful human being. When we are quick to speak our opinions, or to be rude to our friends, or when we interrupt somebody when they are speaking, our inhibitory control is lacking. We can develop this skill by teaching our students strategies that will give them control of their inhibitions. The frontal lobe controls how and when we choose to speak, how we act, the noises we make, and what we do with our body. The frontal lobe helps us to be a good listener, communicator, and teammate.

When your students are having a bad day, are mad or sad, or they are frustrated about something, they act out and cannot always understand why. They may get overwhelmed easily and shut down. It is important that we teach our students to be able to identify how they are feeling and to help them think of strategies that will help them to control their emotions. Executive function skills give you the ability to make a decision no matter how you are feeling. When these skills are developed, students can more easily determine their actions based on their feelings. They are also more likely to bounce back when their executive function skills are developed.

You can help your students understand and control their emotions by teaching a series of lessons about emotions. Many school counselors have specific curriculums for this. Executive function skills enable a student to function even though they may be feeling sad or mad or nervous. They enable a student to control how they are feeling. Social-emotional lessons help students to understand the emotions of others in relation to them. Both types of lessons will help your students and are so very important in the learning process.

The more emotionally healthy a student is, and the better equipped they are to understand emotions, the better they will handle the stressors in life that will get in the way of their learning and success. In my years of teaching with SLP Kathy Tobias, she created mini-lessons for her assigned students. She taught these lessons in our class to the whole group. The students were highly engaged, learned from each other, gained empathy, and learned how to take control of how they felt. These lessons were so good for our students. Sure, they took a little time, but right before our eyes, our students were growing!

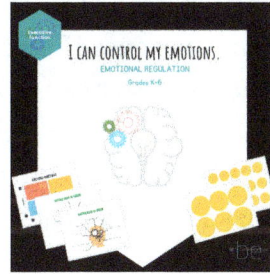

Identifying Emotions

A student can understand how they are feeling and express how they feel. You can teach them to read facial cues on posters or in books to help them understand how to identify emotions. Many curriculums use the Zones of Regulation designed by Leah Kuypers. These are colors that identify emotions—e.g., I feel red (angry or mad) today, or I feel yellow (excited) today.

Many students can do this on their own. However, when we take the time to teach them that emotions matter, they will learn to handle their own emotions and the emotions of their peers in a positive way. You can use a mood meter by having students point to the place on the mood meter. They can share with their group how they feel and also share why they are feeling this way.

Expressing Emotions

Take time to practice sharing how you feel. Give them scenarios from stories or pictures. Have them express how the situation makes them feel. Reassure them that the way they feel is okay and real. It is okay to feel mad. It is not okay to hurt others with your words or actions when you are mad. This is when we start to understand that we have control over our actions. Emotions are normal and our students should know that however they feel, we can coach them through it and they can make good choices.

Identifying Triggers

Brainstorming can help students identify triggers for different emotions. Ask students what makes them feel happy, sad, angry, or excited. Have your students identify the way they feel on a given day and have them explain what caused them to feel that way. They can practice by saying, "I feel _____ because of _____." A simple way to do this is to just go around a circle and take turns saying, " I feel _____ today." If they can share why they are feeling this way it's even better. For example, "I feel excited today because I'm going to visit my cousins!" or "I am angry today because I stepped in a puddle and have a wet sock." Sometimes we can use this information to help turn their day around. For instance, one kid just needs to get a dry sock—easy fix! I know it's not always that easy, but sometimes it just is!

Creating an Emotions Rainbow was one activity that was really powerful. It took just 20 minutes and is well worth the time. We made a big rainbow on a bulletin board. After identifying our mood for the day, each student wrote their name on the rainbow color that matched their mood. This led into the lesson for the next day about responding to emotions.

Reacting/Responding

Share with your students the different strategies for responding to how they feel. Brainstorm ways to get yourself back to happy. Some students may say playing with their favorite toy or stuffed animal will make them happy. Some may say a snack, a hug, or alone time is what will make them happy. It may seem so simple, but when a child's frontal lobe is still developing, they really do not have the skills to think in this way. When emotions arise, teach the students to think about what makes them happy. They can draw it, write about it, talk about it, or take time alone. We can train them to self-advocate by teaching them to say, "I feel mad when you take my pencil. Next time please ask first."

To build upon the Emotions Rainbow that we created in the lesson about identifying our mood, we also made a pot of gold at the end of the rainbow. Each student was given some gold coins to write down what makes them happy. We put our gold coins onto the bulletin board and covered up our sad or mad names with our gold coins.

Self-Talk

Self-talk is a powerful strategy. When students can identify how they are feeling and identify what makes them happy, they can then learn to talk themselves back to being happy. They can do this by saying things like, "I am good at math, I got this!" or "I get to see my grandma after school and the school day is almost over. I can do this!" My favorite thing to teach my students to say is, "I can do hard things!" When you teach them this, you can model it daily as you go about your own daily work. Make it a point to model positive self-talk aloud so that your students can see how it works for you.

One example I always use right before silent reading is this: I say to my class, "I sometimes feel bored and feel that it is hard to read for the whole silent reading time, but I know that I can do hard things. I know that I can stay in the same place and read for the whole time. I am really going to try to enjoy my silent reading time today." Do you see how that works? That sets me up for a successful silent reading time. Much better than feeling miserable going into part of the day that is tough for me. One thing we repeat often in my class is, "I can control my body, my words, and my actions!"

Grace

Teach your class what it looks like to show grace! Grace is understanding and/or forgiveness even when you know it's not deserved. This is something that even we adults struggle with. When a child messes up or feels sad, give them grace. When you mess up or feel sad, give yourself grace. Model this daily! Talk about it as a class. Be honest about how hard it is sometimes to show grace to yourself and to others. This is a lesson that will take them so far in life. Take the time to teach grace!

Collaboration/Teamwork Mini-Lessons

Collaboration is something that can be learned through providing opportunities for your students to work together. Given the opportunities to play or work together will provide circumstances for the students to work through problems, share, compromise, and build upon one another's ideas. Providing students with the time to do this naturally can be done through recess, centers, play-based stations, and group work. However, I have found that teaching students about collaboration is a very powerful tool.

Group Roles

This is a strategy that I learned while teaching in inclusive classrooms with students on Speech/Language IEPs. Group roles develop executive function strategies by assigning a task to a group, while each student in the group is responsible for a different role. This teaches students how to communicate as a team and how to collaborate in order to complete a task. This strategy involves assigning the following roles to students:

- *Leader*—Gives directions, leads the group, reads through directions for group tasks.
- *Secretary*—Controls the step-by-step directions, checks off the list as they complete the tasks given by the teacher, and reviews the list before turning it in.
- *Supplier*—Passes out the supplies and makes sure they are put away correctly. Also may collect papers and other materials that need to be turned in.
- *Time Keeper*—Keeps track of the timer, gives two-minute warnings when time is almost up.
- *Working Partners*—These are the workers, with no specific managerial job to focus on.

You can rotate group roles each week or you can just save them for when you are assigning group projects. It is important that the students learn the responsibilities of each group role and consistently have an opportunity to conduct each role.

Each role will strengthen executive function skills in a different way. When students are given the opportunity to work in a group, often one or two strong students do the work and the other group members tag along and take credit. When you assign group roles, students need to know that they have to work as a collaborative team. They must plan, organize materials and ideas, make compromises, control their inhibitions, and be communicators. Students who are provided the opportunity to work in this manner have a one-up on those who have not. These are the kind of qualities that will help our students succeed in the real world. These are skills that we should be working to help them develop and mature throughout their educational career.

Classroom Procedures and Tools That Develop Executive Function Skills

Morning Routine

Have a clear morning routine for your students. No matter what grade you teach, you need to have a morning routine posted on the wall where everyone can see it. One way to show a process is by using a flow chart. Flow charts provide a visual to remind students of a process. The pictures below are examples of Morning Flow Charts that can be used in any grade level.

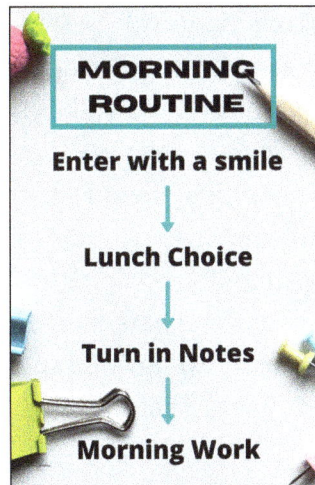

On the first day of school, it should be your goal to show them exactly how to do this routine. Use the 3 Ms (Model, Monitor, and Measure) to teach this process. Start with modeling the routine for your students. Model it the right way more than once, showing them the end goal of being ready for their day. You can sit in a ready position and ask them, "What did I do in order to be ready for my day?" They will tell you the steps that they observed you do. As you work backward you can refer to your flow chart that you have hung in your classroom. Next, you can model it with a missing step (be goofy, make it fun!). Ask the students to tell you what you did wrong. Then model it again, the right way!

Let the kids give it a try. This is where you get to monitor their understanding and progress. I personally like having one group try it at a time so that the class can help me monitor. Then you can talk about what each group did right and how it could be better the next day. This will take much repetition and a lot of time. It will feel like you are wasting so much of your first day, but I promise you, if you take the time at the beginning to get the strategy right, you will be making the rest of your mornings so much easier and productive. This daily practice will create good habits and promote the development of organizing, planning, focusing, and working memory!

There may be some students who continue to struggle with this many steps. That's okay! I have used a Velcro strip on the student's desk to provide them with their own list. You simply have them laminated, cut them apart, and have the student move them onto the strip of Velcro each morning. As they complete each step, they tear it off the Velcro strip and put it away. This will help your students gain confidence each time they complete a step in the morning routine while developing the planning and organizing part of their brain.

Daily Visual Schedule

"Is it lunchtime yet?" "When will I see my mom?" "When is it time to go home?" These are constant questions from students in elementary school. Early elementary students are unable to sense time passing or understand how a given amount of time feels as it passes. If you tell them 30 minutes, they do not understand how 30 minutes feels. This is because the frontal lobe has only just begun to develop. As they access the part of their brain that helps them sense time, they will develop a better understanding of how time passes and what that actually feels like.

For this reason, using a visual schedule can work more like a to-do list of your day. Each day you simply walk your students through the different parts of their day. They will see what needs to be accomplished before lunch and again after lunch. They will learn to understand what time feels like when they've made it through the tasks of the day several times using a visual schedule of their day. With the repetition of going through this visual schedule every day, you will notice your students gaining a better understanding of how long their day is and all the parts that make up their day. Hopefully, this means you will also notice all of their questions involving time and the day's schedule slowly coming to an end.

There are many different ways to use your visual schedule. Most teachers do have a schedule posted in their rooms. However, many just hang it there as a reference for whoever decides on their own to use it. In the younger grades you can use your visual schedule to break your day up into smaller chunks—for instance at the beginning of the day and after lunch. This will break the day into shorter segments for your students. Another strategy is to use a pocket chart so that you can flip over the card that shows the tasks you have completed. Flipping over the cards will help students shift their attention to the next task and give them a sense of time management and accomplishment. It will also work as a visual of how much has been completed and how much is left to complete that day. An understanding of how time feels as it passes will develop and strengthen as you continue to model for your students how the visual schedule can be a tool that they can use on their own.

In the upper elementary grades, you can have a student helper build the visual schedule for the day. This is a great way to begin modeling use of daily to-do lists. As we all know, there are times when our schedule may change based on how the students did with getting things done. It's okay to change it. This will provide an opportunity to help students learn how to manage time and make smart choices about putting the most important tasks ahead of the others. There are so many ways that a visual schedule will help develop your students' executive function skills, leading them to becoming better time managers.

In middle school and high school, when you are only with your students for one period at a time, you can still use a visual schedule to keep your students on track. When they walk into your class, they will know exactly what is expected, get right to work, and understand how much time they may need for each part of the class.

Here is an example of a visual schedule from an 8th grade Social Studies Class:

Today in Class:

Question of the Day

Break-out Session

Class Discussion/Lesson

Explorations

Reflections/Assignments

When a schedule like this one is posted in a middle school or high school class, your students can be better prepared for their time with you. It helps them to stay focused and will prevent down time and time wasted.

Visual schedules can be used in all grade levels. They will help you stay organized, as well as help your students stay organized. If you spend the time to create a visual schedule and put it up in your class, you might as well refer to it and use it as a teaching tool. Strategies like this will develop and mature the frontal lobe where executive function is controlled.

Agenda/Planner

Making a plan for your day keeps you focused and helps students to communicate with their parents about their day. The planner is similar to the visual schedule, but the planner travels home and back to school every day. This allows the students to keep track of what actually happened throughout their day and any responsibilities they may have before the next class.

I've seen planners and agendas used in many different ways. It will depend on the grade level that you are working with. Kindergarten students obviously will not be able to keep a planner. In kindergarten, using a one-month calendar is a great strategy. This can be kept in their folder that they use each day for home-school communications. I recommend having the students mark their calendar each day to report home about how their day went. I've seen teachers have them report behavior, write homework, and use it for teacher notes. This calendar-style planner will work as a great communication tool between home and school.

Keeping a planner or student agenda is a great strategy for teaching your students to be organized with their learning and to plan accordingly. The purpose of this is to write down what you plan to accomplish throughout the day and to give it a time frame. This helps to hold us all accountable for getting everything done in the amount of time given. It also gives our brain a head start on planning, organizing, and focusing. It gives the student a preview of the day. It also gives parents a snapshot of their child's school day.

Each day when your students arrive, have them write down (copy from the board) the daily plan. This will help your students' brains to plan and organize their day. One strategy is to have the students circle the items that will be homework. This will keep them organized at home and keep parents informed.

Another great idea is to invite the parents to write down any commitments that their child may have in the evenings—for instance, clubs or sports. This will help the student make a plan for getting homework done based on the activities they will be attending in the evening.

This daily practice of planning out their day will become a habit that will lead your students to successful planning as they transition into middle school, high school, college, and on into their adult life. To this day, I make a list of what needs to be accomplished each day. I check off my list as I go. I need this daily strategy to keep me focused on my daily tasks. Your students will be more likely to adopt this good habit because you chose to be intentional by teaching this process to them and requiring that it be done daily. This strategy will be appreciated by parents and students alike.

Wipe-Off Analog Clocks

The use of an analog clock provides a visual for students, and it also creates a better sense for time management. All classrooms should have an analog clock. Although students do not typically learn to tell time until 1st grade, using an analog clock in preschool and kindergarten to show the amount of time

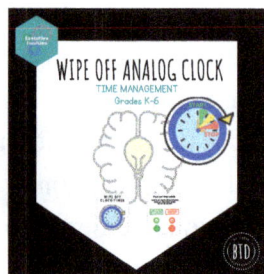

they have to work will create a better general understanding of time. Students in the beginning years of school should know what an analog clock is and see that it tracks time. Let's face it, most of us have more digital clocks in our homes than we did in the past. However, every classroom should have an analog clock to be used as a visual in primary classrooms. This familiarity will make learning to read the clock easier to master when the time comes. The students may even figure it all out on their own based on how you use it to show time passing. The analog clock can easily be used as a visual for time management.

Let's take a look at how to use a wipe-off marker and an analog clock to keep time in your daily lessons. Sarah Ward and Kristen Jacobson have come up with an amazing Time Tracker Program that teaches students how to track the amount of time that they are given to complete a task. In an article called "Staying a Beat Ahead," they explain how they use the clock to do just that. If you tell your class that they have 15 minutes to do a writing activity, you show them what that looks like on the wipe-off analog clock. You simply point to your clock and tell them what time it is. Write the word "Start" where the minute hand is and "Stop" when the time you give them is up. So, in this example, it is 3:00 p.m. and the students have 15 minutes to complete their journal page. Their task is to draw a picture, then write about their picture.

1. Using an erasable marker, shade in the first five minutes and tell the class to use the first five minutes to draw their picture.

2. Then, shade in the next five minutes and tell the class they should use the next five minutes to write their sentence.

3. Finally, shade in the last five minutes and tell them to use this time to check their work, make corrections, and add details to their drawings. It is always a good idea to give them a one- or two-minute warning before their time is up.

There are a couple ways to do this. First, if you are able to take your analog clock down from the wall, you can simply draw on it with a wipe-off marker. This is the best way, because the students can see the minute hand moving toward the mark you made to indicate their stopping time. If you do not have an analog clock in your classroom, ask your principal if there is an option for purchasing one for your classrooms, as they are fairly inexpensive. You can also print off a generic analog clock, have it laminated or put it in a plastic sleeve. This will enable you to draw on it with a wipe-off marker. This is also a great tool to provide for parents to use at home.

Students do not need to know how to tell time to use this method. They will benefit from seeing the amount of time they have to complete something and the amount of time that has passed. Essentially, you are teaching them to manage their task based on the amount of time they have to complete it. This, my friends, is executive functioning in practice!

Teaching strategies that develop the executive function skills in the regular education classrooms might just be the most important thing you teach! This is especially true in elementary school classrooms because it's the prime age for this part of their brain to develop. Without executive function skills students are more likely to be distracted, unorganized, lack ability to initiate a task, and be impulsive. I want to help you gain an awareness that many students will not develop these skills unless they are intentionally modeled, monitored, and measured.

You will, of course, have students who naturally have a strength in the area of executive function, and you will have students who struggle. The goal is to model for students the idea that, just as we can learn to do new things with our bodies, like a dance move, or learn new content like new letters of the alphabet, we can also learn new strategies for our brain. Executive function skills are self-management skills. If we develop the ability to self-manage before diving into academic rigor, our students will be better equipped to achieve success!

Reflect & Consider

1. Consider your current class. What areas of executive function could benefit your students most?

    _____

    _____

    _____

2. What strategies from this chapter do you plan to implement into your classroom?

    _____

    _____

    _____

3. Can you think of a way that you could support the families of your students in working to develop their child's executive function skills?

    _____

    _____

    _____

Chapter 4

Growth Mindset

"With the right mindset and the right teaching, people are capable of a lot more than we think."
—Carol Dweck

H ave you ever really sucked at something? I mean, let's face it, we all have that one thing we tried once and failed at it, and maybe got made fun of or felt embarrassed about it. I'm willing to bet you didn't just naturally have a desire to try it again. For me, it's running. This stems back to elementary school when we would have to run a mile each year for our physical fitness test in gym class. Because let's face it, if you can't run a mile, you aren't physically fit, right? Ugh! I can't even explain how much I loathed this day each year. I was the last one to finish and it hurt. It hurt to run as much as it hurt to finish last. This was when I decided that I just wasn't able to do it. I decided as a 4th grader that if I cut the corners and walked as soon as I felt the tiniest bit miserable, it wouldn't seem as though it was so hard. I know, I know, it makes no sense.

Then in 8th grade I gained a little confidence through cheerleading. We ran at every practice, but not a mile—not even close. My gym teacher that year would "motivate" the slow runners by shouting out, "Let's go, you fluff chicks, pick up the pace." Seriously, this is a true story. This killed me. She had me labeled. Well, there was a group of us (fluff chicks, as she called us) and it really, *really* bothered me. Why even try to run when I would just be called names?

Now, I don't know if this bothered any of the others the way it bothered me, because I never spoke of it to anyone. My mind was made up. I WAS NOT A RUNNER AND NEVER WOULD BE! This gym teacher instilled in me that my feelings about running were spot on—"I just wasn't a runner." When it came to running, even the thought of it left me with a sense of defeat. Carol Dweck calls this a fixed mindset. A mindset that causes us to evaluate situations with thoughts like, "Will I look stupid when I attempt this because I'm not a good runner? Will I be accepted or rejected? Will I feel like a winner or a loser?" This is my own personal example of me as a kid, a young girl with a fixed mindset.

Many years later, my friend Sam's sister, Lindsay, passed away after a heroic battle with breast cancer. Little did I know that attending her funeral would be the event that created a shift in my own mindset. I had only met her sister once, but at her funeral, I was completely inspired! This beautiful young lady was portrayed as a true illustration of strength and determination. She climbed mountains, hiked forests, ran in races, and traveled the world, all while receiving treatment for cancer. I sat in that church and listened to the stories about how she convinced everyone around her that she was still capable of setting and achieving goals, enjoying life, and keeping up this full and fruitful life that she lived. It was that day that I realized this girl had achieved more goals with cancer than most of us without cancer even set out to accomplish.

This way of thinking made all the difference for Lindsay. If she could do so much with cancer, surely I could prove to myself that I could do hard things as well. I pondered this and wondered what in my life was something hard, something that I didn't believe that I could do? Run!

That day, I became a runner! I decided that I would set a hard goal and I would achieve it. My goal was to run a 5K every month of the year for one year. My 7-year-old son and my neighbor were my coaches. I planned to run every other day. My first day out, I just wanted to see how far I could go. My son rode his bike next to me. I ran and ran and ran and when it started to hurt, I continued to run. The app on my phone alerted me, announcing that I had reached one mile. I can still see the corner I was at. I stopped to look at my phone and my son stopped next to me and said, "Mom, why are you crying?" I didn't even realize that I was crying, but oh my gosh, I had done it! I had actually run a mile. I told my son that I had just accomplished something that I never thought I could do, and it actually wasn't as hard as I thought.

That was the first of many runs with my son riding his bike alongside me. My goal was to just beat my distance each time I went out to run. It took me several months to work up to a 5K. However, I am proud to say that I *did* run a 5K every month that year. My son eventually decided to quit riding along with me and learn to love running too! He completed his first 5K that year. What a joy for us both!

You see, if you have a growth mindset, you're able to approach any goal in a whole new way. The problem is we too often train our brain in the wrong way. Let's unpack that a little. Let's learn how we can be the difference in the students we come in contact with. Do you want to be the teacher calling kids "fluff chicks," making them feel like they aren't capable? I think not! I dare you to dig deep into understanding how you can teach your students about having a growth mindset. I guarantee instilling a growth mindset in your students will take them further in life than any academic standard that you are responsible for teaching!

Chapter 4: Growth Mindset

During this time of changing my own mindset, I was observing my own son struggle a bit with anxiety in school. I mean what does a 1st grader have to be anxious about, right? Well, he was anxious! Luckily, his teacher was a firm believer in teaching a growth mindset to her kids. "Growth mindset" was the newest buzz word at the time. Our school staff did a book study called *The Growth Mindset Playbook: A Teacher's Guide to Promoting Student Success.* This book shared strategies that could be used in the classroom to help students understand how to have a growth mindset. And guess what? The strategies worked! My son was an example of how teaching the right strategies can make all the difference in how students feel about their learning.

I've done lots of research about what it means to have a growth mindset. Dr. Carol Dweck has done some amazing Ted Talks and has written several books sharing her own research about mindsets. I recommend doing some research of your own. I would venture to say that, like it did for me, it will ignite something in you that will change your own way of thinking. You will understand the importance of starting to train our kids to have this mindset too!

What is Growth Mindset?

Growth Mindset is a way of thinking and understanding that our brains are constantly growing as we learn. It's how we understand our own abilities and use those abilities throughout the learning process. Dr. Carol Dweck is best known for her research in student and family attitude toward failure. She has come up with the terms "fixed mindset" and "growth mindset" to explain how a person thinks about accomplishing their goals. Dweck shares that a growth mindset teaches students to understand how they learn and how the effort they put forth will determine the success they find. Developing this kind of mindset plays a key role in student motivation, confidence, and achievement in all areas. It will actually boost their ability to achieve! Who doesn't want that? So, let's get down to it.

We should consider two important things:
1. Students can learn to control their attitudes about learning and accomplishing goals.
2. Students can learn to control the amount of effort they put forth.

Our attitude and effort are established from our past experiences. We learn about attitude and effort by seeing it modeled by those we are closest to. When I was a little girl, my dad would play motivational cassette tapes (yep, I am old, I listened to cassette tapes!) recorded by a man many have heard of, Zig Ziglar. I remember on one of those tapes, Zig Ziglar said that each morning before you get out of bed, you should clap your hands three times above your head and say out loud, "Today is going to be a GREAT day!" I remember debating with my dad about whether or not this would really work. So, we tried it—and it seemed to work!

In most cases, it is our parents or the people we spend most of our time with who influence our mindset. Our students each have different past experiences and different perspectives modeled for them. Thinking back to my own personal journey with running, I may have been the only 8th grade girl who was negatively affected by the gym teacher calling us "fluff chicks." My past experiences with running may have played a role in that. Similarly, up until the point of entering your class, your students have learned what attitude and effort mean to them thus far. You have the power to be the one person who gets it right for them.

I once had a teacher who said, "Can't is a bad word." She would constantly repeat, "If you think you can, you can. If you think you can't, you can't!" This was her way of sharing how to have a growth mindset. We cannot control the perspectives of others, but we can be a role model and provide the proper tools to the families who have children in our classrooms. All of this will determine the mindset of our students. Will your students leave your classroom with an understanding of their own mindset? Will they have a fixed or growth mindset?

We can foster learning by teaching our students that they have the ability to control both their attitude and effort for learning through developing a growth mindset. Then we celebrate with them along the way. We celebrate the tiny achievements and the big achievements. We celebrate our mistakes so that we can easily move on to be better. We celebrate the good attitudes. We celebrate the effort! But in order to teach this, we must practice it and model it ourselves. Often, our students form good habits and perspectives at school and are able to go home and share those attitudes and perspectives with their families. This can have a tremendous effect on the family culture.

Why Teach Growth Mindset?

Did you know there is a phenomenon called neuroplasticity? It's true! Neuroplasticity explains that it's possible to rewire the brain. That is right. YOUR BRAIN IS A MUSCLE that will work better when it's used over and over and over again. Dr. Carol Dweck suggests that we teach students that the brain forms new connections when we practice using it, just like the rest of our body. If we want strong muscles, then we practice using our muscles and moving our body, for instance by lifting weights. The same can work for turning negative situations into something positive. Our brain "muscle" will begin to memorize that practice. For this reason, we can change how we respond to challenges throughout our day, especially in regard to learning.

Let me give you an example: Ricky (3rd grader) was not passing his multiplication fact tests. He couldn't move on to x4 until he passed the x3 timed test. We all remember those tests, right? Some of us loved them and some of us hated them. I noticed that Ricky was crying as I collected his multiplication fact test. I stopped and asked him what was wrong, and he said, "I'm no good at multiplication! I am no good at math! My dad says nobody in our family is good at math. I will never pass the x3 test."

Ugh! Doesn't that break your heart? You see, Ricky had the mindset that he couldn't do it. It's like that old saying I learned from one of my teachers: "If you think you can, you can. If you think you can't, you can't." This saying and Ricky's mindset are both perfect examples of a *fixed mindset*. Ricky believed that it was a family trait to be bad at math, and that was that! He accepted it as fact. This belief was holding him back. Honestly, with this fixed mindset, is there even a reason to keep trying? The answer is, of course, yes!

After a good hug and some reassurance, I told Ricky that I understood how he was feeling. Our students need to know that they are not the only people who have to face challenging times. I told him that *anyone* can pass these tests if they believe they can and put forth the effort. You have to first attempt in order to achieve. He didn't quite believe me, so I gave him a strategy to try: I told him that I didn't want him to pass the x3 test tomorrow. (We did this one-minute, timed test every day). I explained that when we have a BIG task, we need to work toward smaller goals. Ricky could do the x0, x1, and x2. I was happy he recognized that because I was going to point out to him that he already passed those sets of tests, and that this was proof that he was able to pass a multiplication test. So, I told him that when we took the test the next day, I only wanted him to focus on getting the facts that he already knew correct, plus 3 x 3. We repeated over and over 3x3=9, 3x3=9, 3x3=9. (I had a very wise teacher in high school who told me when we practice something an odd number of times, our brain is more likely to remember it. I think she just wanted us to practice more than twice, but there is truth to repetition creating memory!)

Throughout the day, every time I would go over to Ricky, I would have him repeat 3 x 3 = 9. Before I hugged him goodbye at the end of the day, I asked him to repeat it again. I also challenged him to ask his dad what 3 x 3 equaled. The next morning, as I greeted my students at the door, Ricky walked up to me and said, "Good morning, 3 x 3 = 9! I'm ready for the test today!"

Chapter 4: Growth Mindset

Ah ha! Ricky was ready for his day because he was ready for his x3 timed test! He knew that the small goal that we had set for him was reachable. He was proving to himself that he was capable. He had a completely different attitude about it because he felt confident, positive, and the big achievement of passing the whole test wasn't his main goal! Tackling the process was where Ricky was going to find his success on that day.

We did this every day until he moved on to the next level. We did it every day until this process became a habit—until neuroplasticity went to work! You see, Ricky's dad seemed to think that their whole family wasn't good at math, so neither was Ricky. But what Ricky's dad didn't understand is that Ricky learned to have a different mindset than he did. Ricky was developing a growth mindset.

I love this story because it illustrates perfectly the difference between a fixed mindset and a growth mindset. In this illustration we watched neuroplasticity in action. We can do this exact thing for all of our students. Before you know it, they will look at daily challenges with a new perspective and hopefully carry it on throughout their lives. This, my friends, should be our goal in education. Not the end goal but tackling the little goals along the way with a positive attitude and effort. We can train our kids' brains before they create bad habits, and we can rewire their brains to change the bad habits that have already been created. Either way it's a game-changer in the success that they will find in school and their lives.

We have learned that neuroplasticity is a real thing. But it starts first with you! Our minds can in fact be changed. We also know that every student who enters our class comes to us with different prior experiences, different abilities, and different strengths and weaknesses. All of this makes each case unique in itself. You are the common denominator. You will be the model for each unique student to develop his or her own growth mindset. But first, you must work on your own mindset!

Developing a growth mindset is important for learning and achieving. The way we think about the situations in our day-today life will develop as we walk through the experiences that life throws at us. When we help our students to develop a growth mindset, they will be more likely to take academic risks. Carol Dweck explains that when we adopt a growth mindset, it doesn't remove the old belief system; rather, they coincide. For this reason alone, it's important that we continue to develop a growth mindset until it outweighs the old belief system within us. The development of this type of thinking will allow our students to know that failing is not the end result. Rather, it is an opportunity to learn about the task at hand. They will gain a positive perspective on setting goals and be able to value the process of achieving their goals both big and small. Having a growth mindset allows students to believe the following:

- I can do hard things.
- I can have a positive attitude.
- I can be grateful.
- I can believe in myself.
- I can be mindful.
- My effort can be the key to my learning.
- I can and will take action.
- I learn each time I fail.
- I can make a difference.

Students who have a growth mindset will believe in themselves, gain confidence, gain endurance to apply effort, and create a more well-rounded, happy, and healthy mind. Having a healthy mindset is part of building a strong foundation for learning. This area of developmental growth will enable students to build positive relationships with others and with themselves. This positive mindset will enable students to outperform those students with a fixed mindset. When students believe in themselves and feel good throughout the process, they will achieve!

Students at all cognitive, physical, and emotional stages or levels can develop a growth mindset. The student who has a high intelligence but gives up when effort is necessary will benefit from developing a growth mindset. The effort is what gets the results that will prove to them that they can do it! The student who is average will also benefit by consistently growing academically and plugging away in a positive way. In my opinion, the low-achieving students and those with deficiencies or delays will benefit the most. Growth mindset is intended to help close the achievement gaps we see with our struggling students. We can show our students that focusing on the process of learning with effort and a positive attitude will help them achieve. Celebrating the process as they reach small goals will lead them to success in the end. Knowing you can and celebrating it is so powerful! This kind of thinking has the capability of completely changing school and family cultures for the better.

How Do We Teach Growth Mindset?

Okay, so how do we teach Growth Mindset? Well, we teach our students through PRACTICE, EFFORT, AND PERSISTENCE. We can train our brain muscle to gain a positive and healthy mental ability to handle situations. Throughout a student's educational career, we can provide them with a chance to form good mental habits. We can do this by providing them with opportunities to practice, put forth effort, and be persistent. This is how the phenomenon of neuroplasticity shapes their minds in a positive way! This even works for grown adults. Anyone can retrain their brain for positivity. You just have to be willing to do the hard work.

Consider the following definitions:

Practice—to teach or train through repeated action; doing it over and over again.

Effort—the use of physical or mental energy, the act or result of trying to do something.

Persistence—to continue to do something in a determined way.

Notice that all of these definitions are action words. So, what do we need to do? TAKE ACTION—do something! We need to find opportunities in our school day to integrate the idea and philosophy of growth mindset into our daily interactions, lessons, and practices. We can train our students through repeated actions (practice), using physical or mental energy (effort), over and over even when, and especially when, tasks are difficult (persistence).

There are many different curriculums related to growth mindset available for school districts to purchase. However, you can develop these skills without having a curriculum at all. I have found nine key themes for teaching students about having a growth mindset and there are nine months in a school year. One idea is to simply teach one theme per month, or you could take the first nine weeks of school to focus on them. Dr. Carol Dweck developed a workshop that lasts eight weeks, teaching students all about their brain, how it works, and how it can be changed. You can read about this in her book, *Mindset: The New Psychology of Success*. Her research showed that this type of instruction proved to make a difference in students' attitude, their amount of effort, and willingness to persist. Another idea would be to set up your own workshop within your own classroom.

You should be taking steps to develop a growth mindset daily. It needs to be part of your routine! The first step is getting your students to believe they can have a growth mindset. This happens through positive thinking. Some people were raised to be positive thinkers—you know those "glass half full" kind of people. But I would venture to say that for many, thinking positively does not come naturally. In order to become a glass half full kind of person, you must intentionally practice positive thinking daily. You must practice until it becomes a habit. Research shows that forming a new habit takes at least 21 days. This means that if you want to form the habit of positive thinking in your students, you will have to take a full month of teaching to practice positive thinking daily. I've got some ideas for you about how to do just that!

A Daily Dish of Gratitude

The idea is that if we start our day off thinking of the good things we have, we can carry that positive attitude into the rest of our day. By identifying what we are grateful for *every day*, we will start to create a habit of looking for the little things that happen throughout the day that we are grateful for. Each day, we should reflect on the day before and try to find the little things that made us smile. It's great to say, "I'm grateful for my house." But it's even better to say, "I'm grateful for the flowers that Ella picked for me from her front yard. They really put a smile on my face." Looking for the little things and being very specific is much more meaningful. I've gathered some ideas for promoting positive thinking that can easily be implemented into your classroom on a daily basis, no matter what age or grade you teach.

Gratitude Journals

Journaling at the beginning of the day is a great place to begin. The most successful people in the world have strong morning routines. Start your day right by having your students write/draw and label things they are grateful for each morning while you are taking attendance and getting them unpacked and ready for their day. This gives the students a positive start to their day. Also, allowing time for students to share is a great idea! You can sneak in some grammar checks and find teachable moments while the focus is on developing a positive perspective.

You can do this in a regular spiral notebook or student writing journal that your district has purchased. Below are examples of gratitude journal pages that are included in the free resource packet mentioned in the front of this book. There are different versions for the different age groups to choose from.

DATE _____	DATE _____	DATE _____
		Today I am grateful for. 1. _____ 2. _____ 3. _____ 4. _____ 5. _____
Draw and write what your are grateful for. I am grateful for _____.	Draw and write what your are grateful for.	Write 3 sentences about one of the things your are grateful for today.

Whip-Around-Pass

This is a game that should only take 3-5 minutes. You have your class sit in a circle. You choose somebody to begin, and they simply say one thing they are grateful for that day. Then they turn to the student next to them to signal that it's their turn—they could even say "your turn," or say the student's name. You go all the way around the circle until you get back to the beginning. This is a fast-paced game. They should not take time to pause and think. You can give them a prompt before you start so they do have a little think-time. The more you play it, the faster it will go! This is a great way to start off your day. It can be used during your morning meeting, to begin or end a lesson, or it's also great to end your day on a positive note. You can also use this game to practice specific academic skills and for getting to know each other. You simply choose the skill to be your topic: nouns, adjectives, sight words they can read from the word wall, anything really! This game also gives your class an opportunity to practice speaking and listening skills. The speaker needs to project and speak clearly while the rest of the class is listening by making eye contact and focusing on the speaker.

Writing Center

You can use your writing center as a time to reflect on all the good things. The students can make a gratitude list or write/draw about one thing they are grateful for. This could be a center that never changes, or you could just use gratitude journaling in your writing center from time to time.

Gratitude Wall

Make a wall in your class or on your door for students to post "gratitude graffiti." The students can write on it (like graffiti), or they can put a sticky note or tape a paper to the wall each morning. I saw one teacher who had made a big white heart and the kids filled it with bright colored gratitude squares until it looked like a mosaic. Another teacher used this idea to show her students how grateful she was for them during her experience with remote learning. Each student emailed her something they were grateful for, and then she wrote it on a sticky note and formed a heart out of all their gratitude. The kids loved it!

Providing an opportunity for our students to use their brain in this way each and every day will eventually form a very positive lifelong habit. Creating the habit of daily gratitude will allow for a shift to a positive mindset. This will allow them to more naturally have a positive perspective when a task they encounter is challenging or time-consuming. They will then be more likely to put forth the effort needed which will lead them to accomplishing the task. When we accomplish our tasks, we build our confidence, which gives us the drive to be persistent. Find ways every day to implement a daily dish of gratitude into your classroom!

Express Your Gratitude

Tell others that you are grateful for them! This part takes a little more effort. This is different from the idea of a Daily Dish of

Gratitude because it's not just a reflective piece. Sharing words of gratitude requires reflecting, but it also requires going one step further and expressing it to the person you are grateful for. Students may struggle with this at first because they may be nervous or shy. The effort comes in building the confidence to tell somebody. There are several ways to teach your students how to express their gratitude to others.

Model It

Tell the kids that you are grateful for them and explain to them why. Modeling this to your students and showing them how to do this properly is key! For several weeks before you teach your students about expressing their gratitude to others, you will need to be the model. Each day, find something you are grateful for and express it publicly to the class. For example, you might say, "Friends, I just want to say how grateful I am for the smiles that I'm looking at right now. When I come into class in the morning, it's your smiles that help me have a great day." Or you can tell the class about something specific that one person did that you are grateful for. "My mathematicians and readers, I just noticed that Benjamin hung up the coat that was lying on the floor. I'm so grateful that you are such a great helper. Now we won't trip over that coat! Thanks, Benjamin!" The students will start to notice this, and they too will look for things that they can point out to others. When they are used to seeing this happening in your class, they will be more likely to express their own gratitude to others.

Teach It

Make a visual to hang in the class! Have the students discuss how they think they could "share gratitude." There are many ways, for example: use your voice, write a letter, say thank you, or give a hug or elbow bump. Have students share how they would feel most comfortable expressing their gratitude to others.

Take Action

Give students different opportunities to show gratitude. Some ideas might include writing a letter to a community worker saying thank you for what they do, or writing thank you notes to friends, bus drivers, school employees, and parents. You can do this as a whole group as well as encourage students to do this on their own for others. However you do it, just do it!

There are so many different ways to share words of gratitude. The more intentional you are about prompting them to do this, the more likely they will start to do it on their own. We are simply coaching them to do what is healthy and good for their own mindset. Some fun ways to do this are listed below.

Pay It Forward

Changing grade levels is a lot of work, as I'm sure you know. The year that I moved from 2nd grade to kindergarten there was so much to do! I spent so much time printing, laminating, cutting, and organizing centers and games in order to build up my supply of grade level activities. In our building our librarian did all of the laminating and we would get our roll of lamination when it was finished and it was our job to cut it out. One morning I found all of my lamination already cut out to perfection and in a bag ready to be organized and put to use. This happened several different times. As I asked around to see who was behind this kind act, what I found was that I was not the only teacher in our building who found the same gift outside of their classroom door. As the year went on, many of us started cutting out lamination as an act of kindness. It was so nice to get to school and find that a very time-consuming task was already done for you.

When somebody does something kind or when you feel grateful for something, try to find a way to pay it forward. It doesn't even have to be to the person that you were grateful for. Just exchange one act of kindness for another. Random acts of kindness bless others, but we learn that it feeds our own minds with joy and positivity. The more we do this, the more we put neuro-plasticity—shaping our brain muscle—to work!

You've Been RAK'D

Get creative! Let your kids brainstorm ways to do this as a whole class and as individuals. Kids love a challenge! Make a class, grade level, or school building challenge for showing random acts of kindness. One amazing teacher does this each year during the holidays. Her class calls it "You've Been RAK'D." She makes cards that say, "You've Been RAK'D" and her students leave the card with the recipient of the Random Act of Kindness. This created a domino effect when another class decided to join in and pay it forward! We never did find out who was responsible for the domino effect of cutting lamination for other teachers in our building, but it certainly created positive vibes and gratitude within our staff. Even though I didn't know who to thank, I think that person knew I was grateful when they saw the domino effect of kindness they started.

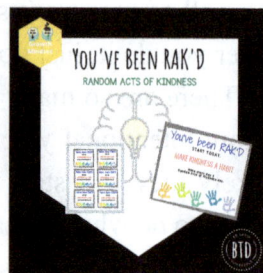

> *"Show your kids that we can be kind, so others will feel gratitude in their lives. It will come full circle because in turn your own mindset is changed for good."*
> —*Anonymous*

There are plenty of resources available that are easily implemented into your classrooms that will teach a growth mindset. Your district can adopt or create a curriculum to use so that you are on the same page with your grade level teams, school building, and/or school district. However, once you have learned what it means to have a growth mindset and why it is important to teach it, you can easily integrate it into your daily conversations, lessons, and activities. A growth mindset will benefit your students and prepare them to handle the challenges in striving for academic achievement, as well as help them navigate their way through life. This growth mindset will enable your students to have the courage to take academic risks and welcome failures as learning opportunities.

Reflect & Consider

1. Do you have a fixed or a growth mindset?

   _____

   _____

   _____

2. Do you practice a daily gratitude routine?

   _____

   _____

   _____

3. Consider what you learned from this chapter. What strategies do you plan to implement into your current classroom?

   _____

   _____

   _____

CHAPTER 5

Motor Skills

Motor Skills are one of the developmental areas that we just assume most kids have developed before entering kindergarten. You and I both know what happens when we assume! If you have ever taught kindergarten, you will know that motor skills, or lack of them, will make or break your day.

I'd like to start with a story about a fellow colleague of mine, Mrs. M, whom I admire so much. Mrs. M. taught 2nd grade and was always wanting to grow so that she could be the very best for her students and for her colleagues. She loved her students. She loved her job. She loved experiencing new things. Each year, she chose a teacher in a different grade level to swap classrooms with for the day. Now, Mrs. M did this for several reasons. First, she wanted to be reminded of where the kids came from and what they would be experiencing in the future years. Second, she wanted to evaluate her own placement and make a decision about whether she wanted to stay put or try something new. Finally, Mrs. M. knew she would always have a lot to learn, and who best to learn from than the students of other fellow teachers! Mrs. M. was reminded from this practice of what her own best practices were and what new elements she needed to include into her own classroom.

One year, Mrs. M. decided to trade classrooms for a day with a kindergarten teacher in our building. They both left their lesson plans and materials out and ready for the other. Mrs. M. knew that kindergarten would take more time and patience—after all, she had raised three kids of her own. She knew that "Kinders" were not as independent as the 2nd graders that she was used to. She was right—those sweet adorable little Kinders kicked her butt! By the end of the day, Mrs. M. was frazzled, her hair was a mess, her tights torn, and she looked exhausted! She responded at the end of the day with the biggest hug for her co-worker and said, "I don't know how you do it! I feel like I didn't teach them a thing! I spent more time zipping, tying, opening and shutting glue bottles, locating materials, problem solving, and helping them navigate through their day than I did teaching. They are constantly moving and need help with everything!"

This is where I chuckle! I laugh every time I think of Mrs. M. and Mrs. W. trading classrooms that day. It wasn't that Mrs. M didn't teach them anything. It was just a different type of teaching. Most of what the Kinders needed was developmental strategies, such as working on their motor skills.

You know, administrators and elementary educators are only trained minimally on the importance of motor development. It seems that motor development is only provided by a school district if a child is significantly delayed and has an IEP to support it. But unless you have actually taught a primary grade, you wouldn't realize that some of our students cannot even unzip a baggie at lunch or zip their own jacket. When you hold the hand of a kindergartener, you can tell by the firmness of their grasp if they have good motor skills. Do you hold your students' hands? You should! Listen, I know they are germy, but that is what soap and water are for. Hold their hands! It will tell you so much. If their hand feels mushy, as most do, they need to work on their motor skills. You will find that every child in your class has a different level of strength in those tiny muscles. This is also true for larger muscle groups. Do motor skills show up in your state standards? They don't in most.

What Are Motor Skills?

Motor skills are actions that involve the movement of muscles in the body. They are divided into two groups: gross motor skills and fine motor skills. Gross and fine motor skills typically develop together because many activities depend on the coordination of both types of motor skills. However, refining the fine motor skills will improve the coordination that will be necessary for larger movement and skills. Let's start with defining both Gross and Fine Motor.

- *Gross Motor Skills*—Abilities that allow people to do things that involve using the large muscles in the torso, arms, and legs to complete whole-body movements (basically, movement of the larger muscle groups).
- *Fine Motor Skills*—The small movements of the hands, wrists, fingers, feet, toes, lips, and tongue. Fine motor skills require working the smaller muscles that help us to hold, move, and manipulate things.

Motor skill development begins at birth and continues to develop and mature throughout a child's life. All children develop motor skills at different rates. By the time children start kindergarten, they typically have developed a good amount of their gross motor skills, as well as their fine motor skills. However, these skills are still strengthening and maturing.

Why Developing Motor Skills in Elementary Grades is Necessary

In primary grades a student's motor skills have so much to do with how they get through their day. If you have had any experience around elementary-age students, I'm sure you know that students in the lower grades (K-2) are much more dependent upon the teachers to help with simple tasks such as zipping coats, tying shoes, handling their baggies in their lunchboxes, and so on. This is not new news to anyone. This reason alone tends to scare teachers from wanting to venture into the world of primary education.

In the early elementary years, when a child's fine motor skills are still developing and/or lacking, classroom tasks can be difficult, resulting in delays in many aspects that are necessary for learning and functioning in the school environment. For example, students may start their day already frustrated because they were the last one to get unpacked. They may choose not to eat their lunch because they aren't able to open a container. Or they may shut down when it's time to write, because they cannot yet hold their pencil and/or it hurts their hand and fatigues them quite quickly.

Lack of fine motor skills can affect how students learn. It can affect how they think and feel about learning. It absolutely affects their mindset about the kind of learner they are. The development of their motor skills really can make or break a student's achievement.

I observed 3rd grade students taking a timed math test to earn a sticker. They had to correctly complete 40 multiplication facts in one minute to earn their sticker. The sticker would go up on a chart. Out of 25 students on this particular day, five did not pass the one-minute timed test. As I observed these students, I noticed that they didn't get one single answer wrong. They didn't pass the test because they lacked fine motor skills. Some wrote numbers using incorrect strokes, which slowed them down. One 3rd grade girl readjusted her pencil grip between each math fact. Several of these students used a very odd pencil grasp. Can you see how motor skills were preventing them from passing their weekly timed math fact test? Three of the five students who didn't pass asked me if they could try again. They each tried three times without finding the success they were looking for.

An article in the *American Journal of Occupational Therapist* called "Fine Motor Activities in Elementary School Children: A Replication Study" examined the motor and technology requirements of kindergarten, 2nd grade, and 4th grade classrooms. The study found that students spend up to 60% of the school day performing fine motor activities, with handwriting accounting for up to 18% of the day. It certainly makes sense that a large portion of the school day includes fine motor work. You can see how a student with weak fine motor skills may feel frustrated and in turn develop a lack of confidence in their abilities.

This study also found that fine motor skills were integrated into tasks throughout the day, including transitions to and from the classroom, and between activities—tasks like unzipping a backpack to get out paperwork for the teacher, gathering materials, managing writing utensils such as pencils and markers, activities of daily living (zipping and buttoning jackets for recess), and technology use (using a finger to participate on a Smartboard). All are included in the school day, and these tasks require the development and integration of fine motor skills.

Unfortunately, the way that public schools are staffed and funded doesn't allow for all students to be provided with the expertise of an occupational therapist. Likewise, regular education teachers are not always professionally trained on the proper strategies for building different fine motor skills. In addition, because fine motor development isn't written into the state standards, many school districts do not require teachers to place a focus on motor skills development. I have found that, unless a teacher has a personal passion and/or gained an understanding from their own research and experiences, motor skills are left to chance. What I mean by this is that we just assume that as a child grows, so will their motor skills. But we cannot make this assumption. The fact is that if we choose to assume motor skills will develop on their own, there will be a percentage of students left feeling frustrated and fatigued with learning. Since we do not want this for any student, we must understand the variables that play a role in motor development.

Motor skills begin to develop at birth and continue on into childhood, and there are many factors that play a role in their development. We all know that babies and toddlers hit developmental milestones at different times and at different rates. The same holds true for fine motor development. Every child in your classroom will have different developmental needs and they will grow and develop at different rates. However, we have seen fine motor development instruction decline in the past decade, overall. This is happening for several reasons:

Academic Standards

Our own mindset in the educational field and in society in the last couple of decades has been "a race to the top" for academics. We are all in such a rush to move on, know more, do more, and to be the best district, school, teacher, and student. We all feel the pressure! So, we have pushed the academics and let the developmental areas—whether we realize it or not—fall behind. I can't tell you how many times I've heard administrators say, when we implement a new best practice, "Something will have to go. You can only fit so much into a day." Well, my friends, how do you decide what needs to go? Is there a way to get creative and integrate things so that you do not have to let developmental needs slip through the cracks?

Pace of Life

Our lives have become so fast-paced that our babies and toddlers are out and about in their strollers and car seats much more than they are on the ground moving and developing. This could be one factor explaining why we are seeing more and more delays in children's motor development by the time they start school. This is not something that we can change or control, but it is something that we, as educators, should be aware of so that we can plan to implement even more motor development strategies to support the cause.

Preschool Attendance

We are seeing more and more children who do not attend preschool. Preschools provide rich environments for learning and developing. It is the one place that kids can learn through intentional, planned-out developmental play. Preschools are oftentimes quite expensive and not mandated in most states. So, in an attempt to save money, many families are not sending their kids to preschool at all.

Kindergarten Entry Age

When to send your child to kindergarten is a big topic these days. We have more and more 4-year-olds starting kindergarten than ever before. The readiness age can be debated, however, and so can the purpose and philosophy of what Kindergarten is and should be. Decades ago, when most kindergarten programs were half day and play-based, it wasn't a big deal to send a 4-year-old to kindergarten. It was, in fact, developmentally appropriate for many. Today the rigor of kindergarten is totally different and not as developmentally appropriate for a 4-year-old. These developmentally young kids starting kindergarten today can seem to be lacking developmental skills such as fine motor skills, in comparison to the older kids in the class.

Gross and fine motor development must be, and can easily be, implemented in the elementary school years. These muscles are crucial for everyday activities such as getting unpacked, zipping coats, organizing personal space, holding a pencil or crayon, and gripping and manipulating objects. It is not only certain students with delays who need this work. Especially in pre-K and kindergarten, *all* students should be working their gross and fine motor skills on a daily basis. In the upper elementary grades, students also need to be given time to work those big and small muscles. Getting oxygen to their muscles will help them focus on their school work.

Developmental skills can deeply affect the input of academic standards—which in turn will affect students' future academic achievement. For this reason, it is vital that developing and practicing fine motor skills be added into our daily routines within our classrooms! Lucky for us, this is so easy to do, and the kids love it!

How to Develop Motor Skills in Your Classrooms

Practice, practice, practice! Daily muscle work! This may look different in every classroom and for each individual teacher, depending on the grade level and student make-up. Motor skill development does not have to take up any additional classroom time. If you are intentional about implementing motor work into your schedule and regular daily routine your students will reap the benefits. The following are some very simple ways to help students develop their gross motor skills.

Gross Motor Development

Recess

C'mon! Everyone loves recess, right? The playground is the easiest place for students to work on their gross motor skills through play—swinging, climbing, running, jumping—and the list goes on. Did you know that kids who can do the monkey bars typically have good handwriting? During recess, watch what your students choose to play. Encourage them to do the activities that will strengthen them in the right way. You can be intentional about playing the right games or activities that will help your students develop in the areas necessary.

Brain Breaks

In the classroom, you can intentionally implement gross motor work into your regular brain breaks. GoNoodle.com provides brain breaks that kids really enjoy, including activities such as dancing, exercise, and stretching. However, you can do this without any tools at all. You can have students run in place as fast as they can, press their hands together while they focus, and sing songs with movement and memory motions. Any time they are stomping, climbing, crunching, and lifting, they are using gross motor skills.

Academic Areas

When you are intentional, you can implement gross motor movement into any part of your learning day. For example, kindergarteners could form letters with their body, count by tens while doing jumping jacks, or stomp out their spelling or sight words. There are so many ways to do this! You simply need to be intentional. Upper elementary kids can jump or dance when they hear a particular vocabulary word. Drama and dance can also provide gross motor work for your students—have them act out a story plot! I think you get my point: Get the kids using their muscles. Bust a move, people!

Crazy Maze Hallway

Many elementary schools are turning their hallways into a maze of sorts that provides opportunities for gross motor work, while serving as a break from the classroom. As the students move down the hall they follow zig zags, hop on dots, spin on circles, and so on. This has been a trend more recently and creates a fun environment for developmental learning.

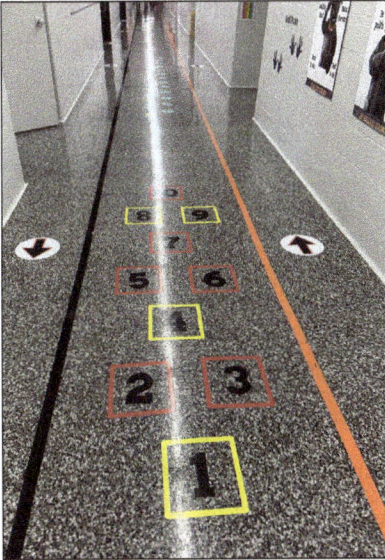

Fine Motor Development

Fine motor skills practice should be part of the daily routine in elementary classrooms as well, especially pre-K through 2nd grade. You can plan for fine motor workouts in your daily lessons using strategies that will simultaneously work those tiny muscles in the wrists, hands, and fingers as they learn their academic content. This is easy and also will make learning fun!

In upper elementary grades (3rd – 5th) the need for this daily practice will be less. However, we all know that from year to year our case load is different. There are years when there is more of a need for it than others. When teachers see a need, they provide those kids with the strategies and activities that are necessary for learning. The same holds true for fine motor development. If you have students with developmental delays, you will know how true this really is. If you have a handful of kids with weak fine motor skills, will it hurt to assign the whole class spelling word practice using playdough or putty? Absolutely not! In fact, sometimes bringing out the "little kid toys" brings learning back to life for those upper elementary kids. Let's face it, there is a kid in all of us who is dying for an opportunity to play!

Now, let's talk about how we can do all of this without adding more to your plate. We can easily integrate motor skills into the parts of your day that are already established. While teaching in inclusive classrooms for many years, I had the opportunity to work closely with our building occupational therapist. She would typically take her assigned students to her office to work on specific areas that were written into the individual's IEP. The therapist would meet briefly with me to explain what she is working on. Oftentimes, she would come into the classroom to observe her assigned students. She would share with me the strategies that she was hoping to see carry over into the classroom.

I learned so much from watching her work with my students. She taught me strategies for pencil grips and how much pressure was needed when moving the pencil across the paper. I would often take these strategies and turn them into mini-lessons. She also shared with me some ideas for tools to use throughout the day to help with motor development. I plan to share all of this with you, but first I want you to think about where it will all fit in. You see, there is not a lot of extra time to kill in today's classroom. Rather than adding another thing, let's sneak some motor work into something you already do.

Consider the following:
- Write down your daily schedule.
- What do your students currently do when they first arrive at school?
- Do you have any type of centers in your daily routine?
- Do you have a time that the students are in a free choice station?
- Consider your language arts and math time.

While teaching in inclusive classrooms with the intervention specialist and occupational therapist, I observed them using tools for motor development in their daily language arts and math lessons. What parts of your day could you use tools for motor skill development?

Fine Motor Bins

Daily fine motor work is necessary in lower elementary grades. Fine motor bins are the best way that I know how to do this. Basically, you create a rotating schedule of short activities that will last for the month. Each day the students do a different bin. This is a concept that many of my teacher friends use in a variety of ways. It's brilliant, really, and can be used at any time during the day. I recommend it to be used first thing in the morning. I believe that we all need a soft start to our day. This is also a way to work "smarter, not harder."

You see, you simply find tubs, bins, drawers, whatever works for you, and you fill them with fine motor activities! I used a rolling drawer unit that had 11 drawers. I would fill each drawer with a different type of fine motor activity. Each morning when the students walked through the door, they started their morning routine, which then ended with getting their fine motor bin. The students knew which bin they were getting and, if they forgot, there was a rotating chart posted in the room. I also recommend assigning them a partner (this also helped with keeping each other on track). Fine motor bins work well first thing in the morning for a couple of reasons:

- *Motivation.* Students love to do them! It motivates them to get unpacked and started with their day quickly, if you use them as morning work. They cannot wait to get into the classroom and start digging into their fine motor bin! They can also be used as a reward. I've even had students ask if they can do them during indoor recess! Sure! Why not?

- *Work Smarter, Not Harder!* No more searching for busy work to use to occupy them while you take attendance and check folders. If you fill at least 10 drawers, this will last a month before you need to refill them. This way you don't have to plan for it every week or every day when you are already implementing the daily fine motor work as their morning work. It's also fun to use monthly themes.
- *Move the Body!* Moving the body (big or small muscles) wakes up the brain! These fine motor workouts will get their little muscles moving first thing in the morning while keeping you on track with DAILY fine motor practice. Using these muscles will wake up their brain so that it's ready to learn for the day.

Weekly Centers

Most elementary classrooms do some sort of weekly or daily center rotation. Designate one of your weekly (daily) centers to fine motor development. This doesn't mean you have to ditch what you already do. It simply means that you keep the centers you always plan, but choose one of them to have an activity that requires fine motor skills! The list is endless. This can be done in any subject area. Fine motor is not the subject area—it's the tool and action used to complete the activity in the subject area.

Extra Activities

When students finish their work, teachers typically have several options for students to work on so that they aren't wandering around or interrupting those still working. A jar of playdough is the perfect quiet activity! Coloring pages are fun for all ages! In the upper elementary grades, one teacher had a knitting table or cross-stitch projects. This is another way to keep the motor skills strengthened!

Individualized Fine Motor Activities

There are going to be students in your class who have developmental delays and may need to work with the school occupational therapist. This is a great opportunity for you to learn from your student! Allow them to use what they learn from OT in your class daily. Celebrate their progress by allowing them to showcase the strategies they've used to accomplish their goals. You can also ask your school OT to suggest strategies and tools that will help you to create fine motor practice for your whole group based on the needs of these individuals. All of the students will benefit, the delayed student will feel confident because they already know how to do it, and you will be supporting your occupational therapist's individualized goals for the child! This is really important and will pay off.

Okay, let's recap! Fine motor development is vital for the long-term success of academic standards. We can integrate fine motor work into our already-established schedule without taking away from another part of our day. We can do this daily, weekly, whole group, small group, and we can individualize it! Now, what types of tools and activities can be used to strengthen fine motor skills? What are the tools that you will put to use during your daily routines?

Tools for Your Classroom

Playdough

I can't say enough about how much play-dough will help develop your student's fine motor skills! If you are teaching early elementary grades, this should be a staple in your classroom. Some teachers give each of their students a container to keep in their desk to play with when they are finished with their work. Another idea is to have a playdough station in your classroom for free choice centers and/or free play. I know several teachers who

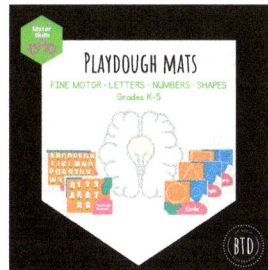

have their students play with playdough every morning when they arrive in the classroom. However you do it, if you can find a way to give your kids a chance to squeeze, shape, and roll playdough every day, they will strengthen their motor skills.

Hole Punch Activities

Squeezing the hole punch works the muscles in the fingers and hands and develops wrist movement, leading to holding a pencil for long periods of time and writing with strong and controlled muscles. Hole-punching activities work on strengthening the muscles in the fingers and hands. Squeezing the hole punch is a hand workout! Students also practice visual motor skills by finding the location to hole punch. Specifically, they practice visual discrimination skills (the ability to recognize the likeness and differences of shapes/forms, colors and position of objects) while working the hole punch by finding the item they are punching out. In addition, the student is able to practice bilateral coordination skills (the ability to coordinate both sides of the body at the same time) by holding the paper with one hand and using the hole punch with the other hand, much the same as scissors. Hole punch activities have always been a favorite for the students in my class. They just love to try out new tools.

Oftentimes, the students find that a hole puncher tends to be more difficult than they look. Students may tire easily and may even attempt to use both hands to squeeze them, especially those students with a delay in fine motor development. These are good to use at the beginning of the year (especially if you are a preschool or kindergarten teacher).

By the end of kindergarten, you should observe progress in the amount of effort a student is able to put into using that hole punch. That said, we are sure to consider the developmental growth made throughout the school year. Not all kids will be at the same place by

the end of the year. However, it's the growth that is important. Can they squeeze with more strength at the end of the year than they could at the beginning? It's all about the growth that they made! There are many fun activities that will pull in the academic content standards. Hole punching is always included in one of my fine motor bins. It is a difficult task at the beginning of the year, but it really builds their strength! In addition, you can also use the tiny pieces that fall from the holes to create designs, sight words, number formations, shapes, and much more! Why not get creative?

Snap Cubes

There are many different types of snap cubes. Often you will get snap cubes with your district's math curriculum. If not, you can order them for a very reasonable price. Anything that you can press together and pull apart (e.g., LEGO blocks, Unifix Cubes, Snap Cubes) will be great for gaining strength in those hands and fingers. These little cubes make learning in the regular content areas so much fun! They provide a tactile and visual way of learning. They can be used in all grades for sight words, spelling words, math concepts, and creativity. These cubes can be included in your Daily Fine Motor Bins. Have them in one of your bins ready for a new activity when it's time. Look for other opportunities to use them as well. If your students need a visual for counting, adding, and graphing, why not use a manipulative that will develop fine motor skills?

Therapy Putty

Raise your hand if you want to dig tiny parts out of putty that is silky smooth? Pick me! Pick me! Who doesn't love to dig and discover? Therapy putty can be used to work the muscles in our wrists, hands, and fingers, too. You can just work it with your hands, or you can make it more purposeful and hide objects in it to aid in learning the academic standards, while creating a sense of wonder and discovery. You can hide small objects to sort, sequence, count, and compare/contrast. Therapy putty strengthens fine motor planning (the ability to come up with a plan and carry out a fairly new motor skill in the correct sequence from beginning to end.) Stretch, mold, and pull the putty until you find all the hidden objects—and then hide the pieces all over again!

Pop/Snap Beads

Toy or tool? Both! This fun tool will have your students strengthening that pincer grasp that is required for holding the pencil with the amount of firmness needed for effortless, neat handwriting. Try it! Right now, put down whatever you are holding and pretend to be snapping beads together. Look at the position of your fingers. That's it—the correct handwriting position!

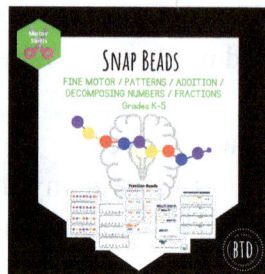

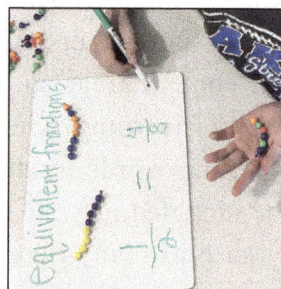

Snap Beads can be used to show patterns, decomposing numbers, adding up and down, and just for fun! Make Snap Beads one of your daily fine motor bins and/or pull them out to help with instruction or assessing in the content areas. So many possibilities! Yes, students will consider this tool a toy. They will make a necklace or bracelet, no matter how old they are! Chances are they may even wear it! Let them play! We learn through having a desire to play. We are motivated to complete tasks that are fun. We are proud when our play creates something cool and smart. We can work their little fine motor muscles while playing and learning with snap beads.

Lite-Brite

Oh, the nostalgia this toy brings! If you had a Lite-Brite, I bet you never once thought that while you were playing you were actually working a developmental necessity! I'm sure your parents didn't either! Lite-Brite is a great toy for using your smaller hand muscles, visual perceptual skills, visual motor skills, and creative play. Placing the small colored pegs into the holes and punching through the paper requires the same pincer grasp used to hold a pencil. Today, school-age kids are most often found playing video games and swiping a screen, which can both be educational and work those hand muscles. Bring out the Lite-Brite and your kids will be so excited to give it a try! I purchased one for my classroom to try it out. What I learned was that one was not enough. In reality, four to six of these would be great! It works lovely as a weekly center. In early elementary, you can just allow kids to use the black sheets to make images or create images of their own. You can also form letters and numbers or write names and sight words. My students were really into making their word families with the Lite-Brite. It could be used in a daily fine motor bin for building words, shapes, patterns, fractions—the learning is limitless!

Scissors

Rule of Thumb = thumbs up! Always thumbs up! The opening and closing motion used with scissors helps children develop the small muscles in their hands. Using scissors the right way is something that many kids cannot do when they come to school. The typical entry-level kindergartener's motor skills are not strong enough to manipulate the scissors yet. This is why we need to pay close attention to the child's handedness— which, by the way, some may be unaware of—before handing them their scissors. There are also different types of scissors.

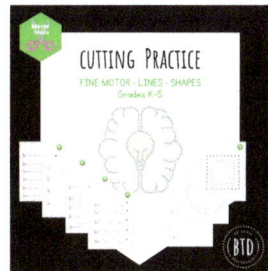

Slow Down! Children Are Learning!

There are some that do not have finger holes. These can be used for students who cannot manipulate scissors with finger holes. They simple squeeze and get the tiny muscle workout needed for strengthening the necessary muscles for cutting. Cutting helps develop hand-eye coordination as children hold the paper with one hand and cut with the other while tracking the movement of the scissors with their eyes. Scissor cutting also helps to develop bilateral coordination. Bilateral coordination involves using both sides of the body at the same time while each hand is performing different tasks.

Do not assume all students will figure out how to hold scissors on their own. Teach your students the proper way to hold scissors. This may seem silly, but believe me, they need this lesson! These tips can be used and explained to students the first time you get those scissors out. I personally think the older kids could use a reminder too!

- *How to hold them while carrying*—Pointy end down and held in fist. This way, if the student would trip and fall, the sharp end is not going to stab anyone! Also, it allows them to hand them off to somebody safely.
- *Thumbs Up*—Whichever hand they use while cutting, the thumb is always on top! One tip is to wrap colorful tape around the thumb hole so children will know where to put their thumb. You also could ask the parents to do this before bringing school supplies into school. However, having your students help you with the tape can be part of the lesson, and they will remember because they are physically doing it. You can also draw a smiley face or put a sticker on their thumb nail. While cutting, they should always be able to see the smiley or sticker.
- *Sharp end points away*—While cutting, the sharp end of the scissors should always be pointing away from you. Use the other hand to turn the paper you are cutting, rather than turning the direction of the scissors.

— 126 —

Do not skip "cut and paste" activities because they take a "long time"! The kids need to practice cutting or cutting will never become more effective or efficient! I know it's faster to have a parent volunteer cut all their pieces and parts ahead of time. I know it's dreadful waiting for kids to finish cutting. However, I also know that we *must* give them this time to practice their cutting skills!

Reflect & Consider

1. Write down your daily schedule and circle the time of the day you plan to implement fine motor work.

   _____

   _____

   _____

2. Make a list of classroom supplies you may need to purchase in order to implement the strategies you learned from this chapter.

   _____

   _____

   _____

3. Make a plan for how you will put what you learned into action.

   _____

   _____

   _____

CHAPTER 6

Handwriting

> *"Handwriting activates a unique neural circuit,*
> *which makes learning easier."*
> —*Dr. Stanislas Dehaene, Cognitive Psychologist*

I taught 3rd grade for eight years. When I first started teaching, we would order cursive review handwriting books. The students loved writing in cursive. However, this was during the time when there was a big debate about whether or not schools should formally teach handwriting. The digital world had arrived, and kids were learning to type in elementary school. Academic rigor was at an all-time high.

I remember sitting in a curriculum meeting and listening to the council of teachers and administrators discuss the importance of learning to type. This quickly turned into a debate on whether or not we should ditch teaching cursive handwriting and replace it with a better curriculum for learning to type. This was the big 3rd grade debate in my school in the early 2000s. Our curriculum director at the time decided that it would be best if we dissected the state standards to see what they have to say about the issue at hand.

At this time, our state standards only vaguely mentioned handwriting. It very plainly stated: *Students will be able to write legibly*. Well, there you have it, folks. This was when our district administrators decided to no longer spend money on handwriting instruction. We went from copying old booklets and handouts, to no longer teaching cursive handwriting at all. I mean all they had to do was write legibly, right? There just wasn't enough time in the day to do it all, so something had to go. Cursive handwriting went right out the window!

Teaching handwriting became a thing of the past. The state standards continued to become more and more complex, giving teachers even more to fit into the school day. Kindergarten made the change from half day to full day, which gave the teachers more time to teach the standards. This was around the time when I moved from 3rd grade to 2nd grade, and on down to my favorite, kindergarten, where I spent the rest of my career. This was eye opening!

It was then that I realized that not only were 3rd graders replacing handwriting for typing skills, but so were kindergarteners. Because most kids came to kindergarten already writing their names, they didn't feel the need to "waste time" teaching letter formations. They no longer had a handwriting curriculum. The reading series offered practice pages, so the district determined that would be an easy way to save money and time.

As the standards in kindergarten changed and got more complex, we started to see that other developmental skills were also getting left behind. We didn't have time to do cut and paste activities, so instead of cutting and pasting, we just colored or circled the answers. Basic lessons on how to properly hold the pencil and scissors were slipping behind, with the assumption that kids already knew that.

Year after year, we continued to hear the upper grades complain about how messy the students' handwriting was and that they couldn't even cut in a straight line. Well, yeah, when you don't teach them how to do it correctly, and allow for sufficient practice time, it will not be as efficient or effective. So once again we met with our curriculum team with our concerns.

This time we asked our occupational therapist to go over the value of teaching handwriting and what the different curriculums have to offer. The committee listened and reviewed the material presented, but surprisingly voted down the idea of going back to a formal handwriting curriculum. The big question was: How can we expect students to write paragraphs when they are never formally taught how to properly hold a pencil and practice the correct movements and formations?

You and I both know that this decision was the wrong one. There is a tremendous amount of research supporting formal handwriting instruction and motor skill development in elementary students. Furthermore, although the standards are becoming more complex, the developmental state of kids entering elementary school is the same. So, believe it or not, the team of teachers I was part of chose to buy their own handwriting curriculum and to implement it.

Teaching manuscript and cursive handwriting in classrooms has become less common in the past couple decades. This has happened for various reasons. First, the increase in digital tools has created a debate among school administrators and teachers as to whether or not teaching typing should replace teaching handwriting. Second, the rigor of academics in the early elementary years has forced teachers to go from teaching formal daily handwriting lessons using a handwriting curriculum, to modeling the basic strokes and moving on. Some administrators and teachers felt that students will "figure it out" as they move and write more. However, more recently we are seeing handwriting making a comeback!

Why Teach Handwriting?

There are many reasons why we should be teaching handwriting in elementary schools. It seems that educators have gotten into the routine of teaching directly to the state standards, and in many states, handwriting is barely mentioned in the state standards. Some states simply require legible handwriting. For this reason, many schools have pushed handwriting aside to create more time for the other learning standards that are more easily measured or that will show up on a test. And yet, teaching proper handwriting will develop areas that may not be measurable on a test, but will aid in future academic achievement overall.

Brain Development

Teaching formal handwriting in early elementary grades actually aids in cognitive brain development. When a student learns and practices letter formation in a consistent pattern, the brain's reading circuit actually sparks or lights up. There is a connection between language development and the act of using proper handwriting strokes. When a student practices writing a letter from top to bottom and left to right, a part of the brain is activated for development. Consistency in doing so creates strong muscles in the hands, making writing effortless. When writing sentences is no longer a physical challenge, students can put forth more effort in the content they are learning about. Students tend to do better at reading and spelling when they have been trained properly to form letters. Forming letters by hand while learning sounds activates reading circuits in the brain that promote literacy. Handwriting aids in cognitive development, thus leading to better developed literacy skills in our students.

The brain will not get the same developmental workout if handwriting instruction is replaced with typing skills instruction. I'm not saying that typing skills shouldn't be taught, but it should not replace handwriting instruction. Handwriting activates the brain more than keyboarding because it involves more complex motor and cognitive skills. Because handwriting is a multi-sensory activity, it contributes to reading fluency by activating visual perception of letters. As you form each letter, your hand shares information with language processing areas in your brain. As your eyes track what you're writing, you engage these areas. The same goes if you say letter sounds and words while you write. Everyone learns best when information is presented in multiple ways. That's especially true for kids with learning and thinking differences. Handwriting is one of the greatest multi-sensory learning tools.

Overall Academic Achievement

Learning to write by hand is a key component in improving both spelling ability and writing applications. Students with labored handwriting often experience a drain on mental resources needed for higher-level writing, including attention to content, expanding on details, and organization of ideas. Teaching handwriting daily in our classrooms is so simple and inexpensive, and yet the benefits of this are extraordinary.

Handwriting can predict later reading success. Handwriting fluency frees the child's mind for more complex composing skills. Even in upper elementary and middle school, learning to write in cursive can improve spelling and composing skills. All of the research on handwriting demonstrates immediate gains and lasting benefits for a child's academic achievement. Teaching handwriting must have a place in the daily curriculum.

Kids need to learn proper handwriting! Can you tell I feel passionate about this? It is such a simple thing to include in your day. You only need 10 minutes. That small amount of time will pay off in so many different ways. You get more bang for your buck when you take the extra 10 minutes!

How to Teach Handwriting

Handwriting is best learned through direct instruction. It is a complex skill engaging cognitive, perceptual, and motor skills simultaneously. Believe it or not, there is a right way to teach handwriting! It's really simple:

- Model
- Practice
- Redirect
- Practice
- Assess

I am a firm believer that kids need to get up and move. I am a firm believer that kids shouldn't sit at a desk and be taught to. I am also a firm believer that kids can sit in a good handwriting position for 5-7 minutes to practice good handwriting! Many think teaching handwriting is "old school," but I'm here to tell you it's not!

In my kindergarten classroom, I looked at my schedule to see where I had an odd extra 10-15 minutes. That is where I plugged handwriting exercises in. There have been years when it's after Morning Meeting, before Silent Reading Time, after returning from a special activity, or right before lunch. However, it really works at any time. I try not to teach handwriting right before a writing lesson or writer's workshop because that is a lot of physical writing for those tiny muscles in the hand. The last thing I want is for my students to feel fatigued when it's time to get creative with writing. Consider your own day. How can you squeeze in a handwriting lesson?

Steps for Handwriting Lessons

1. Have kids spread out around the room for a brain break. I like to use a fun movement song or video to get their bodies moving.

2. While they are participating in the brain break, I pass out their handwriting page. Some years we had workbooks and I would have them get those out before the brain break.

3. I gather the kids on the rug to teach the strokes required for forming the letter. I like gathering on the rug because, it's quaint—just my style! It also prevents them from working ahead and not watching the instruction of the letter formation.

4. Use terms such as: Start at the top line, go down to the bottom line and stop, pick up your pencil and go back to the start, make a big curve down to the bottom, and stop. The terminology that you use may be determined by the curriculum your school follows. It is important that these terms are used from one grade level to the next. Consistency is key!

5. Model writing the letter with perfect "teacher handwriting" and also model writing the letter a few times with mistakes.

6. Call on a student to come up and circle the letter with the best formation. Call on a student to correct each of the mistakes made to the other letters.

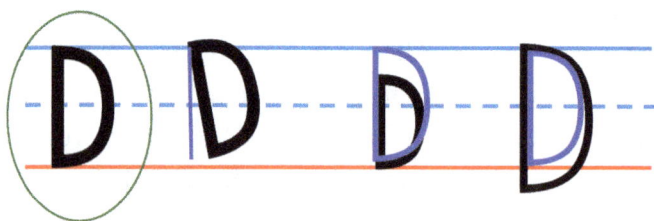

7. Have students repeat aloud the steps to form the letters while drawing it with their finger in the air or on a partner's back.

8. Instruct students to go back to their seat and sit in a good handwriting position.

9. This is the most important step! Have your students circle their favorite letter that they wrote and then as you walk around the room, observe each student forming their letter. Observing each student form the letter is so important. This

ensures that your students are not forming bad habits. When you observe them forming the letter incorrectly, be sure to correct their mistake and have them try it again.

10. I *always* put a star or a sticker at the top of the paper, even if they have poor handwriting! It's the effort and time that we care more about.

This process should really only take 10 minutes. This 10-minute daily practice will have an immense pay-off in the end. Some schools have the philosophy, "If it's not going to be graded or on the test, don't spend too much time on it." This makes my belly boil! This statement is like saying, "Don't take time to teach kindness, because it's not tested." Or "Don't take time to talk to a student who came in crying today, because it will waste instructional time." Can you even imagine believing this way? It's so frustrating. Even though handwriting does not necessarily get a grade—and actually shouldn't—we still need to take the time to teach, practice, re-direct, and assess. Assess does *not* mean grade. It is simply checking in and knowing how to help our students make progress.

Formation vs. Neatness

Handwriting is not busy work! What I mean is, don't take these 10 minutes as a time to sit down and check your email. If you are at your desk, there is no way of knowing if your students' handwriting is simply neat, or if they actually used the correct strokes for the letter formations. Simply modeling, practicing, and assessing isn't enough when it comes to reaping all the developmental benefits of handwriting. When you teach a new letter formation, provide gross motor movement before they even get to the paper pencil practice.

Also provide your students with an opportunity to judge and fix incorrect letter formations. During the practice time, they should be able to trace it, try it, and trace it again. This repetition is important. Once they have practiced, you should watch each student form the letter. This way you know that they are not practicing the wrong strokes. A letter can still be neat and not be formed accurately. What is the big deal, right? *It is absolutely a big deal!* As we learned above, the consistent motions of letter forming will make them more fluent writers. In turn, it will make the whole writing process easier throughout their lifetime!

Consider a Curriculum

There are so many different handwriting curriculums to choose from. Most importantly, get your school district on the same page. Consistency in handwriting terminology and routine is vital for optimal brain development and fluent handwriting. It's best when students begin and progress through the same curriculum as they learn manuscript and move on to cursive handwriting.

When choosing a curriculum, you may consider the following:
- Daily practice
- Not too much or too little
- Starting dots
- Integration of other literacy skills

If your district, like so many others, has tried to save money by not purchasing a handwriting curriculum, you can still teach handwriting! In fact, I'd be willing to bet that most of you reading this do *not* have a district-purchased curriculum that every grade level follows. That is okay! However, I do still recommend that you ask your district's curriculum director and district occupational therapist to help you decide on one as a team, even if you are not going to officially purchase it. You can still follow their philosophy and terminology as guidelines. There are so many supplemental resources that can be used to follow the different curriculums out there.

Essential Handwriting Lessons

Good Handwriting Position

It's not very often that we expect students to sit in their desks properly. In fact, many schools have flexible seating or different styles of seating. In one classroom that I visited, there were not any traditional stationary chairs. The idea of flexible seating is good, but there is a time for sitting properly and handwriting is one of them. Teach your students how to sit with a good handwriting position:

Bottom in chair,
- Feet flat on the floor,
- Back straight and comfortable,
- Forearms resting on the desk.

Sitting Stomp

Sitting Stomp is how we can check to see if our bodies are in good handwriting position. The students sit at their desk in good handwriting position. They will know what this means because it is one of the first lessons we teach them about handwriting. As mentioned previously, they would sit tall in their chair with two feet on the ground and their forearms on their desk. When you say, "Go!" they will stomp their feet as hard and fast as they can—as if they are smashing grapes on the ground. When you say, "Stop!" they will stop and start their handwriting practice. This is a fun little way to begin, it gets everyone ready and in position!

How to Hold a Pencil

Take the time to actually teach a lesson on how to hold a pencil. Then, each time you observe a student holding their pencil the wrong way, simply remind them of the correct way.

There are several acceptable pencil grasps. The chart here shows how to teach the correct way. Many students alter that grasp to what is more comfortable for them. If they are able to legibly make the letters using the correct formations, then let them use the grasp that is more comfortable. However, if they are lacking fine motor skills and have shaky or illegible handwriting, continue to promote the grasp shown here. This grasp provides them with stability needed to write.

Many students enter kindergarten with bad habits already formed. The more you are consistent in correcting these bad habits, the more likely they will be corrected. If you are teaching 2nd grade or a higher grade, you are most likely not going to correct a child's pencil grasp. By the time they reach 2nd grade, they should have strong enough motor skills to hold the pencil. If they have weakened control of the pencil, you should be in contact with your school's occupational therapist for tips and advice.

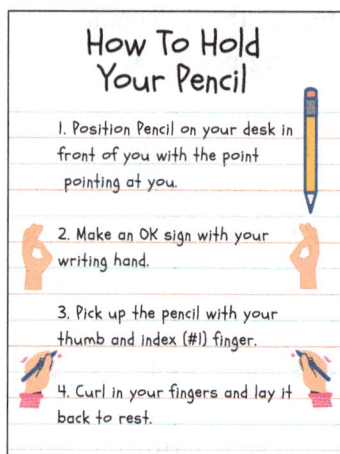

How To Hold Your Pencil

1. Position Pencil on your desk in front of you with the point pointing at you.

2. Make an OK sign with your writing hand.

3. Pick up the pencil with your thumb and index (#1) finger.

4. Curl in your fingers and lay it back to rest.

Tips and Tricks from the Occupational Therapist (OT)

Slant Board

If a student is having difficulty with handwriting, one of the tricks used most often by occupational therapists is a slant board. The slant board helps to ensure good posture when writing. It also helps with extending the wrist so that it is in the correct position for neat handwriting. A slant board can also help if you have students who have poor bilateral coordination skills. You may notice that they struggle with holding their paper still with one hand while writing with the other. There are slant boards that are used by occupational therapists that are at a 22-degree angle.

However, I have found that if you have the student write on the cover of a closed, large three-ring binder, it works just the same. Using a slanted surface also helps with visual tracking. Reading on an angle is easier and it's helpful for students when they need to read what they wrote in order to continue on to the next word. If you have students who struggle with their writing, you may want to pull out a binder and give it a try.

Belly Writing

When you lay on your belly to write, your forearms support your body in the same position that is required for good handwriting. This practice allows your students to strengthen the muscles necessary for writing. It also will help them to position their body properly, which may not feel natural to them while they are sitting at a desk.

Board/Easel Writing

Using a vertical surface is another way to promote and develop good handwriting. It gives the arm and wrist the ability to extend, as well as gives them the stability required for fine motor movement, leading to better handwriting. So, let your students draw on your white board or chalk board. Make a graffiti wall or paint on an easel.

Pencil Grips

There are many options available for pencil grips that slide onto the student's pencil. They range in the amount of support they give to the student. In my experience, students love to experiment with different grips. Each student is different, and it is a matter of trial and error when deciding which grip is best for each individual.

Shortened Pencils

When teaching a child how to hold a pencil, sometimes it feels awkward and uncomfortable. You might try breaking a pencil in half, sharpening it to be 2-3 inches long, or my personal favorite, golf pencils. A shorter pencil is easier for new writers to manage.

The difference is amazing when you see it in action.

Writing in Clay

Use a plastic lid and spread modeling clay into the lid. Have your students use a pencil to make their letter formations. The pressure needed to do this will build the muscles needed for handwriting. Feeling the motion of the letter formation will help students to learn their letters. The same would be true with spelling words and math facts.

Texture Writing

Writing on paper with some sort of texture under it is another trick I learned from an OT. Being able to feel the texture of what they are writing on will help them to remember the correct motions and letters. You can use sandpaper, burlap, bubble wrap, or anything else with a texture.

Finger Tracing Boards

Tracing the letters on large finger boards will also help with memorizing the letter formations. Remember that making the formations correctly will light up the brain!

Reflect & Consider

1. Do you currently take time to teach or review letter formations?

   _____

   _____

   _____

2. What part of your day would you be able to review letter formations?

   _____

   _____

   _____

CHAPTER 7

Sensory Integration

> *"The senses, being the explorers of the world,*
> *open the way to knowledge."*
> —*Maria Montessori*

What is Sensory Integration?

Sensory integration is the process by which we receive information through our senses, organize the information, and use it to participate in everyday activities. We use our senses to navigate through our day. The way we gain understanding of everything is controlled by what and how we make observations through using our senses.

When we choose to teach in a way that uses all of our senses, we are more likely to ensure all of our students learn and understand what we're teaching. When you stop to really think about your senses, I bet you will be able to identify how your senses enhance your learning. For example, smells can often take you back to remember something you did or some place you went in the past. Your sight helps you to categorize groups and remember visualizations that you learn from. Touching an object helps you to understand what it is made of. You see, we need to have rich sensory experiences so that our brain is able to make these connections.

Here is a true story: There was a boy in my 1st grade class who ate his school paste. I'm not joking! He seriously ate it, like all the time. Did you ever know a student who would chew the eraser end of their pencil or eat the pen tops in high school? Do you know someone who constantly taps the tables, clicks their clipboard, and makes noises when they're thinking? Do you have kids who are always rocking or wiggling when they talk? How about students who are always in others' personal space? I personally find that if I read a book, I'm less likely to lose focus if I read aloud. Have you ever met an adult who repeats what you are saying so they can process the information mentally?

Many of us rely more on one sense than others. Our senses can be over-stimulated or under-stimulated. However, we all use our senses every day for learning, processing, thinking, and interpreting the world around us.

Before we can get into how to integrate sensory experiences into our classrooms, we must first be sure that we are familiar with our senses: sight, hearing, smell, taste, and touch. But did you know that there are two others? That's right! There are actually seven senses. Many do *not* know about or understand these other two senses: vestibular and proprioception.

- *Vestibular Sense*—The sense of movement and balance. This helps us to know where we are in space.
- *Proprioception Sense*—The sense of body awareness. This is how we sense where we are in relation to other people and things around us.

These two senses provide information to your brain about your body's position in relation to your environment. Vestibular sense allows us to understand which direction you are facing and how close you are to things around you. This is necessary for respecting personal space, knowing when to slow down when running, and knowing how high a step is before climbing up it. The proprioceptive system tells you the amount of effort being used to move your body (speed, pressure, how hard you press down on your pencil). This sense tells us when to stop, how fast to go, and how hard to push down on something. These two senses work together most of the time. Often one relies on the other. Healthy and well-functioning vestibular and proprioceptive systems are important, just like the other five senses.

Learning about these two senses was a major aha! moment for me! This explains why little kids fall all the time. This explains why they invade our personal space, bump into everything, and talk too closely. If you have ever been able to observe kindergarteners at recess compared to 3rd graders at recess, there is a big difference. The kindergarteners fall down just running, they miss steps, and find it difficult to walk on a balance beam or line, while 3rd graders have better developed these senses. Their bodies are able to move around quickly, balance, understand how close they are to an object, and how hard to push or pull on something. If you teach a primary grade, understanding these two senses will make a world of difference. While these senses are still maturing, we can be intentional about using tools in our classroom to foster learning through these senses.

Why Sensory Integration is Necessary

Think about the students in your class right now. What types of sensory needs do they require for optimal learning? Many teachers think that sensory integration, sometimes referred to as a "sensory diet," is just for students who have sensory disorders. The truth is we all have different sensory needs. Everyone at every age will process information differently, based on how their senses work.

When preparing your learning space, classroom instruction, transitions, procedures, routines, and centers, you must consider integrating different sensory needs to promote success for your students. Providing a sensory-filled learning environment will foster learning for all students. In the past decade educators have found the value in differentiation of learning styles. Sensory integration basically does the same, providing the sensory needs of a variety of students who learn in a variety of ways.

How to Implement Sensory Integration

Classroom Space

The classroom design should be organized and tidy. The walls should not be overly stimulating. Visual displays should foster an environment that is calming and focused. Picture schedules help to provide students with an organized plan for their day.

Classroom Furniture

The furniture you have available in your classroom should vary in shape, size, and comfort level. The buzz word today is flexible seating, meaning that you can move, change, and exchange seating arrangements throughout the day, week, and school year. Many classrooms with flexible seating offer bean bags, stools that wobble, chairs that help you sit up straight, rocking chairs, booths, and yoga balls. Allowing your students to choose their seat is also a new idea in today's classrooms. Having a variety of classroom furniture is great for sensory integration. It also allows you to be able to provide students with a seating option that will benefit them.

Understanding your student's sensory needs is important when offering different classroom furniture. There will be times, as I'm sure you know, that a student cannot handle sitting on different types

Slow Down! Children Are Learning!

of furniture. There will also be times when it makes all the difference in their ability to focus and attend to the lessons. Yoga balls are a perfect example of this. Allowing students to sit on yoga balls at their desk can help many students balance and focus. However, some students cannot handle using an inflatable ball as a chair, and for some students the ball becomes a distraction. With sensory needs being diverse, it's important to understand your students' needs. It's also important to know when to give the student choice and when to assign particular furniture to students. Classroom furniture is a big part of including sensory into your classroom.

Comfy Corner

This is a space where students can relax and/or unwind from stress or anxiety. In this space you may find fidgets, calming tools, books, paper, crayons, and pencils. It is good to have simple calming tools, but not too much to choose from!

There are times when students get overstimulated, which can lead to frustration and oftentimes complete meltdowns. When this begins to happen, we should read the cues from the student and lovingly provide the comfy corner to them. This gives the students time away from the stimuli and time to rest their mind. Some kids do not have the stamina to make it through an entire day. We are seeing kids start kindergarten at younger ages and, to be honest, some are just not ready to be away from home working, thinking, and actively doing for this many hours. The Comfy Corner can be a place for a short rest. On a side note, I've always thought that a whole group rest time was important in the lower grades, especially with how rigorous their day is!

The Comfy Corner should never be used for punishment. Children should view the area as a safe spot and use it when they need a "break." This area should encourage the child to manage his or her state of mind by simply removing themselves from the sensory overload they are experiencing. You will most likely be the one to determine whether or not the student can have time in

- 146 -

the Comfy Corner. However, as time goes on and the students understand its purpose, you may witness students being able to understand that they need time there. You may witness young learners understanding their own needs and learning to self-advocate! This, my fellow teachers, is when we feel good about what we are teaching our students. Truly, isn't our goal to teach kids to understand their needs and to know how to access what they need in order to learn best?

Transitions

Transitions are a prime time for sensory overload. Here are a few suggestions teachers may use to support their students during transitions. Be sure to provide constant cues about upcoming transitions (verbally, musically, visually).

Transition Music

There are many different types of transition music. You can purchase songs that have the purpose of helping students transition from one activity to another. For example, I used to use a song that was two minutes long, started slowly and gradually increased in speed as the students were running out of time. This allowed the students to feel that their time was almost up. Transition music can be soft and calm to lead into a lesson where the students will need to be focused, or it can be upbeat, preparing them to move and get their wiggles out. I personally think that purchasing a set of transition music that varies in purpose is one of the best sensory integration tools that you can integrate into your classroom.

Consistency

Have a couple of different routines for transitioning. Being consistent with transition routines will help the students to sense what is coming next and know in advance what is expected of them.

Visual Timers

There are many different options for timers. Timers that show a visual of the time passing and how much time is left help students to understand the concept of time and time management.

Change the View

Change the view in your classroom to help students understand that a change, or transition, is about to happen. This change in view may mean that you move to a new spot in the classroom before giving the instructions. Move to a new part of the room to teach so that they can shift their focus to something new.

Dim the Lights

Adjusting the classroom lights is another way to foster learning through our senses, when you train your students to know what the different light effects mean. For example, dimming the light may mean that you are going to make a special announcement. You make up the rules for this one. If your lights have a dimmer switch you can get even more creative!

Volume Control

Noise can be very overwhelming for many students. For this reason, it is important to determine noise levels in your classrooms. You can also help your students plan for success with volume control in other parts of their school day by designating volume controls for the cafeteria, library, recess, hallway, and so on. Give your students specific noise levels for specific activities, for instance:

- *Seat Work*—Volume 0
- *Partner Activities*—Volume 1 or 2 (whisper or soft-spoken voice)
- *Centers*—Volume 2 or 3 (loud enough for your group to hear you, but quiet enough that other groups do not hear you)

- *Presenting*—Volume 5 (good speaking voice or teacher voice)
- *Change the volume of noise*—Use your voice to direct the students' attention to where you want it. Teach the students to repeat what you say in the same style and volume of voice that you are instructing them.

Spatial Awareness

Teach your students about personal space. Understand that even after you teach them you must still provide reminders. You can provide your students with visuals and other tools to help them learn to feel and sense what they are doing with their bodies in relation to the classroom and others in it. Some examples of tools that will help your students gain an understanding of spatial awareness are listed here:

- *Tape Markers*—Use tape on the floor to show where students begin their line, sit on rug, or even to mark the space that belongs to them at their table or desk.
- *Carpet Squares or Space Markers*—You can use carpet squares to show students where to sit on the rug or throughout the learning space.
- *Hula Hoops*—Hula hoops are a perfect visual for allowing the appropriate amount of space between you and other objects. These are fun tools for teaching personal space. Teach your students to imagine that they have the hula hoop around them.
- *Store-bought spots or stickers*—There are many products that will stick or Velcro to the floor. You can use these spots in so many creative ways.

Music and Dance

Incorporating music and dances into your lesson can promote learning and attention. Keep your students moving! When you move your body, oxygen is sent to your muscles, making your brain more alert. Movement also helps with memory.

Pencil Variety

Students can use different styles of pencil grips, pencil sizes, and pencil shapes. Whatever supports their individual needs. My favorite pencil is a golf pencil, used by golfers to keep track of their score. Oftentimes a shortened pencil will improve young students' handwriting. The shorter size gives the student more control of the writing tool. Triangle-shaped pencils often promote proper pencil grip. Pencil grips can also be a tool that can promote better handwriting just because they are fun, and kids get excited to use them.

Scented Markers

Who doesn't love to use a scented marker? Smells can promote memory. Have you ever smelled something that took you right back to a time when you frequently experienced that specific smell? For me there is a certain lotion that takes me back to my high school days. The smell of pot roast takes me back to my mom's house! Smells may trigger memories and experiences. If you always use smelly markers to practice spelling, this could be one way that the sense of smell fosters learning in that area. Even if smells do not work this way for you, they are still a fun sensory tool that will motivate kids to complete a task and learn! There are many different scented learning tools out there that will be sure to motivate and engage your students in learning activities. The sense of smell can promote learning in your classroom.

Sensory Bins

Sensory bins promote tactile learning. This gives the students a chance to dig, explore, communicate, and learn. Running your hands through sand, cotton balls, shredded paper, and other materials can be calming. Trust me, even the adults who visit our room can't keep their hands out of the sensory bins. It evokes curiosity! Students are curious and engaged while learning through play at the sensory bin. They are relaxed and having fun when they are at this center. Sensory bins can provide a rich sensory experience that promotes learning.

Note that in order to keep your sensory bins germ-free, the first and last step should be to wash and dry your hands, using soap. This gives your students one extra reason to wash away the germs while providing a clean sensory experience.

Fidgets

Some kids just need to move their hands. Allowing students to hold a stress ball or push and pull a snap cube may help them to focus while not distracting others. Finding the right fidget for your student is the tricky part. You may have to try a few before you find the one that works. It's a great idea to have a fidget basket with a variety of fidgets. This way, as you get to know your students' needs, you can easily experiment with what works best with your diverse students' needs. Having a basket with variety on hand will prevent you from having to dig through your supplies. You can use items that you probably already have in your classroom, or you can buy specific fidgets at educational stores. Your school occupational therapist should be able to help you brainstorm ideas for specific needs. Use the resources that are in your school! Some items that you may already have include stress balls, gum, playdough, pieces of soft fabric (felt), snap cubes, and so on.

Gum

Chewing gum can help students focus. When you tell your class that they can chew gum to help them focus on their learning, it both motivates and soothes them. I must add that you will need to place some rules on gum chewing. For example, if the gum is out of their mouth, it disappears! It can also be fun to have a moment or two after the focused time is over to try to blow bubbles!

Tools to Assess Your Space and Daily Schedule

Sensory Integration Table

Be intentional about planning sensory integration into your day! You can map it out by using a chart or checklist, as shown on the next several pages. Fill out this chart with what you already do in your classroom that fosters an environment for learning. Place it in the column for which sensory need it fulfills. Then get creative and think of new ways that

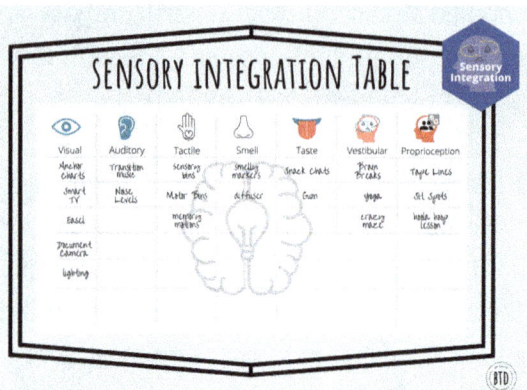

you could fill in the areas that you see are lacking. Which area of sensory integration seems to be lacking in your classroom? This table is a great visual for what you already do and what you need more of!

Sensory Integration Checklist

We must also look at the different times of our school day. Are there certain parts of the day that are over-stimulating? Are there certain parts of your day that do not have enough sensory stimulating activity? For example, in the early elementary years, it is difficult to hold students' attention for a long story.

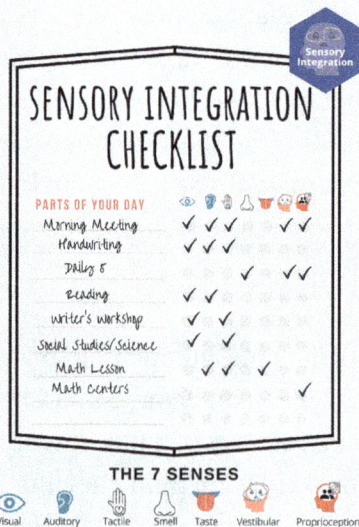

However, if the story is sensory rich (props, sound effects, textures) it will tend to hold the students' attention longer.

This sensory integration checklist can help you reflect on the different parts of your day and how much sensory is integrated. You simply write out your daily schedule and place a checkmark for each sense that is integrated during that part of your learning day. This is a great way to see what senses are lacking and what parts of your day offer the most sensory integration. I think you will be surprised at how much sensory integration is already being offered in your typical day in the classroom. This checklist may also help you to understand why certain students are under- or over-stimulated at certain times of the day.

Reflect & Consider

1. Fill out the Sensory Integration Table found in the free resource packet mentioned in the front of this book. What senses are the hardest to implement? What are some ideas for implementing more senses into your instruction?

   _____

   _____

   _____

2. Use the Sensory Integration Table to identify parts of your day that are sensory rich and parts of your day that are lacking sensory integration.

   _____

   _____

   _____

3. Jot down some ideas for how you want to make your classroom a sensory-rich learning environment.

   _____

   _____

   _____

Foundational Literacy Skills

CHAPTER 8

Foundational Literacy Skills

What Are Foundational Literacy Skills?

There are four basic Language Skills: reading, writing, speaking, and listening. Many English Language Arts Standards have identified the following as foundations for literacy: letters and sounds, phonemic awareness, phonics, print concepts, high frequency words, and vocabulary. These skills must be mastered in order for a student to be considered a fluent reader.

Why Are Foundational Literacy Skills Important?

Students' foundational literacy skills must be strong in order for them to learn to read and later read to learn successfully! It is important that our students have optimal time to *master* (or make concrete) the foundational literacy skills. When a student is able to master and practice these skills until they are able to use them without effort, they will have a firm foundation for learning in all academic areas as they progress in school. Having a firm foundation of these basic skills will allow students to achieve more complex literacy skills as they move on from grade to grade.

How to Teach Foundational Literacy Skills

The answer to this question is such a big one! There are so many wonderful ways to teach foundational reading skills, but in order to properly teach them, we must first consider the following:

- The skills required to be developed in order to create fluent readers.
- The process that is necessary for developing the skills needed.
- The strategies and tools that foster the development and process of becoming a fluent reader.

The Skills

Foundational literacy skills can be viewed as the building blocks for reading fluency. It is said that up until 3rd grade, students are "learning to read." When they reach 3rd grade, there is a shift to "reading to learn." Leading up to this point, we must build these strong foundations for literacy in order to create fluent readers.

Fluent readers understand that letters make sounds to form words that have meaning. Fluent readers are able to make meaning of what they read in order to learn and/or enjoy it! Let's break that down.

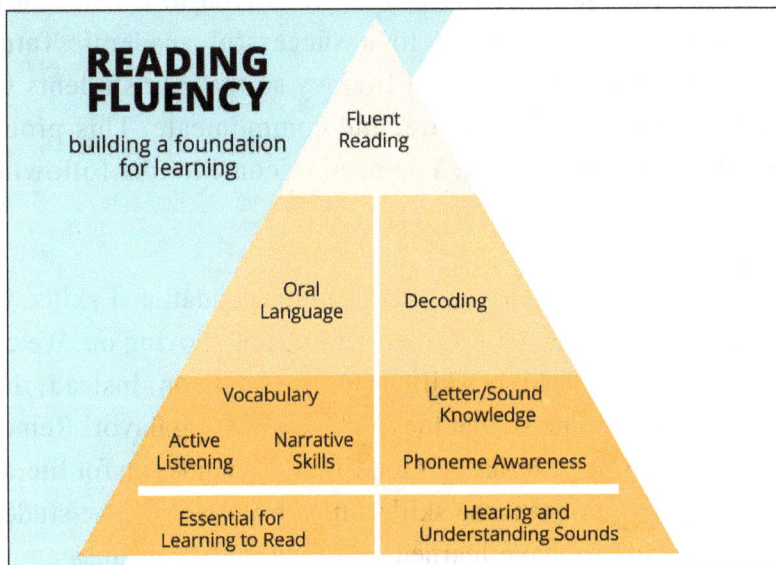

This diagram shows the goal at the top of the Reading Fluency Pyramid: Fluent Reading. In order to get to the point where they can read fluently, a student needs good oral language and decoding skills. Just below that on the pyramid, it shows that you build oral language through vocabulary, active listening, and narrative skills. At the same time, students learn to decode through understanding letters and sounds and have a phoneme awareness. The foundation (the bottom of the pyramid) for becoming a fluent reader is developing the essentials for learning to read and learning to hear and understand sounds. Another way to understand this is through the following formula:

ORAL LANGUAGE
(Vocabulary, Active Listening, Narrative Skills)
+
DECODING
(Letter & Sound Knowledge, Phoneme Awareness)
=
FLUENT READER

The Process

Learning foundational literacy skills is vital to fluent reading and comprehension, leading to a successful academic future. We must build a foundation for literacy so that our students will learn to effortlessly read, write, and communicate. This process should be well planned out. You need to consider the following:

Time

Take your time! When you are teaching foundational skills, it is important that you are not just memorizing and moving on. We cannot have the philosophy of skill, drill, and move on. Instead, these skills need to marinate so that they will have lasting flavor! Remember, the purpose of these skills is to provide a foundation for literacy. Taking your time to let these skills simmer will enable the students to access what they have learned more naturally with less applied effort or thought.

Sequence

The order that you go through these skills does matter! First, you will want to follow the order of the curriculum that your district has purchased. If your district does not use a research-based curriculum, you will want to be sure your grade level teams conduct vertical alignment. This means mapping out specific skills that are being introduced, practiced, and mastered in each grade level, creating an appropriate sequence. This way you are not skipping any of the important areas in helping your students build this firm foundation for reading.

Repetition

Research proves that you learn and form habits through applied effort and practice. This means that in order to learn something or do something habitual, we must apply effort over and over again (practice) until it is memorized or a habit is formed. This is why repetition is so important in learning, especially when building a foundation for other learning skills. If you are teaching pre-K through 3rd grade, you will want to revisit these foundational skills from time to time. You want your students to learn these skills and carry them along throughout their learning. This way, the skills will be built upon, leading to high achievement and drive!

The Strategies and Tools

There are so many wonderful tools that teachers can use in their classrooms to achieve the goal of building a foundation for literacy. My advice is to share with your teacher tribe all the best practices that you use in your class. When teachers share ideas, we work together to make learning more fun and achievable for our students. Another piece of advice is to find a couple of teacher blogs that you love and follow them. Use their ideas to make your classroom an amazing learning environment.

Listed below are teaching strategies and tools that have been used by my teacher tribe! They have been tried and tested by young learners and teachers. You may already use many of these tools, but if not, I hope you will try some of them and enjoy them as much as my tribe has.

Skill and Drill

This doesn't mean drill all day! Skill & Drill should be quick (no longer than 5 minutes) and fun! Skill & Drill should *not* end when a skill is mastered! Even after a skill is mastered, it is good for students to run drills of skills to allow those skills to be made concrete, so that they can access that skill without even trying when they need to for higher level skills. For example, if your class has mastered their letters and sounds, it is still beneficial to find time to go through a practice drill of reviewing the letters and sounds. This is only making the skill more concrete. Skill & Drill doesn't have to be boring, but it certainly can be if it's the only strategy you use for learning a specific skill.

Learning Styles

Understanding how each of your students learn is vital to their finding success in learning. A foundation for literacy will be much more easily accomplished when you consider how kids learn best. You should be delivering instruction through visual, auditory, and tactile learning strategies. All kids need to move! So, teach foundational reading skills through movement! Making up motions or moving around the room while learning will foster learning to read fluently. When you learn through using your senses, your brain makes that learning a memory. So, go ahead, toss out some of those handouts that are boring your students! Let those kids create, draw, dance, sing, and stomp it out. Whatever it takes!

Oral Communication

> *"Reading and writing float on a sea of talk."*
> — *James Britton*

Talk about it. Kids love to talk! They love to hear stories! Tell them about your day and somehow intentionally find a way to sneak a skill in there. For example, maybe you are teaching spelling patterns for long /a/. Tell them a story that will spark their interest. You could even draw pictures to go with it as you tell it. Ask them to listen for the long /a/ sounds as you re-tell the story. This time write the words and then talk about the spelling patterns. Remember that communication goes both ways, so give them a chance to contribute to the conversation. Have them respond with connections they've made or let them add to the list you are creating for the skill you are intentionally practicing during your conversation. You can also provide opportunities for your students to engage in conversations about skills with a peer. As your student revisits the skill or lesson, their brain is able to access, organize, and go further with the information during their conversation together.

Surprising Experiences

Create a sense of surprise! These are the most memorable experiences. You can use puppets, mystery bags, mail deliveries, and the list goes on! Who remembers the Letter People? If you grew up with the Letter People or taught with the Letter People, they are the perfect example of surprising experiences. It was so exciting to meet each one and find out what they liked, color their picture, listen to their song, watch their video, and make motions each time you heard their sound. Wow! Why aren't they still hanging around? They brought surprise, and students couldn't wait to find out what they would learn with their new Letter People. It's kind of like when we adults receive a piece of mail (not a bill, of course!). First, you see who it is from, and still you are intrigued by what it could be. The same goes for your students. The anticipation of finding out is so exciting! Get creative and build their foundation for learning through surprising experiences.

Small Group Reading

This is, in my opinion, the most important form of instruction. You can (and should) change up the way you form your groups based on your goals. For example, instruction in phonics and decoding is most effective when done in small groups where students are grouped by need. However, if your focus is on reading strategies (making predictions, facts and details, drawing conclusions, re-telling) you may want to have a heterogeneous grouping so that the weaker students have role models in their group. The make-up of your group can be entirely up to you. What should be done during your small group reading?

- Review high frequency words that will be found in the text.
- Reading for a purpose: Introduce the book with a question or prediction, do a picture walk, state the purpose for reading the book, and/or read the book aloud together.
- Practice a phonics or decoding skill.

- Talk about what they learned or read about. The value of small groups is connecting through conversations about the book.

Read Aloud

There is research and evidence that show the benefits of a child being read to! If a child is read to for just 15 minutes each day, they will reap benefits that are exponential for learning.

Read Aloud at School

Opening up the world through storytelling helps the students gain an understanding of the world around them. You can use read-aloud stories to teach character traits, problem solving, and academic skills. By modeling good reading strategies while reading aloud to your students, you can show them how to use the strategies of a fluent reader. Their imaginations can go to places that will help them begin to understand and infer. Plus, kids love being read to! There is a bond that happens when you read to a child.

Read Aloud at Home

I know you have no control over what goes on in the homes of your students. However, I also know that parents are a big part of holding their kids accountable for doing their homework. So why not give your students a "listen to a story" homework assignment? You can share the benefits of reading aloud to a child, and then assign a story each night. Parents sign off on reading logs all the time, so why not have them log the hours their child listens to stories?

Free Choice Reading

Free means free! This means no rules! Let them read whatever they want for free choice reading. If a child is intrigued by a book that is far beyond their reading level, so what! Any book, any time is my philosophy. Promoting self-motivated reading will help establish a true love for books and reading.

District Curriculum

Hopefully your district has adopted a research-based scope and sequence. This is important so that from grade level to grade level your students are learning all the skills for building decoding skills incrementally.

Systematic Instruction

If your district does not follow a research-based scope and sequence, then it is up to you to create it. Systematic instruction in phonological awareness, phonics, and sight words is necessary for students to become fluent readers. It has been proven to accelerate students' reading development.

Reading Bags

This is a tool that will provide *leveled reading practice*. Each student is given a reading bag (this can be a simple gallon size zipper bag) where they keep several books at their level. This bag will travel to and from school each night. The purpose is to constantly be listening to and reading books that are just right or even a little bit of a challenge. The student should read the book three times before it gets returned to school. In order to return and replace the book, they must read it to you or to a parent or classroom helper. Students need to do a high volume of independent reading in increasingly challenging books. I used a plain old spiral notebook to keep track of each student's bag of books. When they read it aloud to somebody, the title and level would get written down on that child's page. This can be used to show growth at conferences or even just to encourage the child throughout the process of progressing through reading levels.

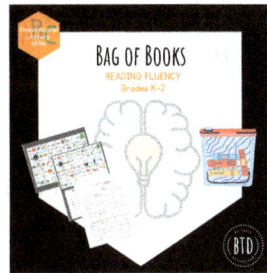

High Frequency Word Program

Most reading curriculums have their own way of introducing high frequency words. You should use this process so that they are applying the knowledge of words to the texts they are participating in. However, I highly recommend an additional, motivating, and *fun* way to practice high frequency words. Contests are a great way to do this. Another way to do this is by simply doing a quick check every week. When the students expect to be tested on the words, they will be more likely to practice them. You should break down the high frequency words into smaller lists. Have the students practice their lists until they are mastered. These lists can be used during centers, at home, during morning work, or even free time. Use fun tools to motivate them and celebrate along the way! Celebrate any and all progress.

Word of the Day/Week

Place the word of the day/week on a special board. The students can try to use it in their writing and read it each time they walk past it. Seeing a word in isolation will allow the students to gain a concrete understanding of the word. You can use, for example, sight words, basic vocabulary words, feeling words, and complex vocabulary. One teacher I worked with would wear the word of the week around her neck on her necklace. The students couldn't address her until they read the word she was wearing. Another teacher would write words on handprints outside of her classroom door. Every time a student entered the room, they were to give the handprint a high five and read the word. It was like their special code to get into the classroom. In upper elementary, you can introduce a complex vocabulary word for your students to learn and use all week long.

Songs and Nursery Rhymes

Music and rhythm might just be the key to understanding phonemic awareness. When we sing, we learn to predict the pattern of sounds in words and phrases. Our brain is signaled to understand what makes sense and what does not make sense, based on the rhythm and rhyme. Rhyming and discrimination of sounds is one of the main key concepts of building a foundation. Songs, poems, and nursery rhymes are the best way to build your students' phonemic awareness. Who cares if you can't sing? The students love music. Music is catchy, easy to remember, and it will make all the difference! So, sing, sing, sing your little hearts out!

Peer Reading/Coaching

This is when kids get to read and/or coach each other. Pair your students so that a stronger reader is partnered with a weaker reader. Teach several lessons showing the students what your expectation is for peer reading. Show them how to share the book and read loud enough for their partner to hear them. Teach them how to coach each other along the way. This will need lots of modeling and monitoring. Have simple routines that are consistent and remain the same all year. Teach your students to repeatedly say "good job" to each other! I recommend traveling around the room during this time to check in with your peer readers. This will prove to be an effective strategy for building reading skills and fluency.

Book Clubs

If you're not in a book club of your own, then join one or start one! There is nothing better than hanging out and sharing a book! I promote book clubs for all ages. Have students work on a book of interest or a specific level with a group of peers. This is something that parent volunteers could help you with. This is a great way to provide students with a chance to have conversations about storylines, characters, feelings, and more! Let's make reading fun!

Mystery Readers

This is when you secretly plan for a guest to come in to read to the class. I've seen teachers do it many different ways.

- *Special Student Days*—Plan for a family member or friend to come in on birthdays or student of the week. This sense of surprise is so exciting for the whole class, but especially for the student being featured.
- *Reading Weeks or Events*—If your school celebrates Right to Read Week or features a book fair, this is a great way to promote fun with reading. Simply ask for volunteers to come in as a surprise.
- *Monthly*—Scheduling one or two mystery readers each month is an easy way to organize it. You plan for it at the beginning of the year and put it in the calendar!

Building Stamina for Silent Reading

Give your students a time of the day (preferably every day) to read silently. In the primary years you will definitely have to work up to an appropriate amount of time for silent reading. In my kindergarten classroom we started with three minutes. When you master three minutes, you celebrate—and I mean really celebrate! Kids need to feel good about their achievements, and every tiny milestone matters. Increase their time by one minute each time they master it! These little achievements will result in big achievements. Our end goal was to be able to be independently enjoying their books for 15 minutes each day. When you reach your goal, celebrate! The books that your students enjoy during this time should not have any rules on them. They should *enjoy* this time! Reading is fun!

Literacy Centers

There are many different ways to create literacy centers. Many different methods have been researched and evidence has found that kids love center time and it's the best form of practice! It doesn't matter how you organize it, just do it! Your centers should allow students to move, play, manipulate, and learn. It's a bonus if you include different ways of learning to promote all learning styles. It's an added bonus if the kids don't even know they are practicing learning skills! I've heard teachers say, "Kindergarten and 1st graders can't handle centers." That is absolute *hog wash!* What they cannot handle is sitting all day, listening, and regurgitating information. Primary kids *can* handle centers and *need* centers for concrete and meaningful learning.

Shared Writing

When your students begin to write, give them a lot of opportunities to share their writing. They can share with a peer, with the whole class, with you, with anyone really! It's so good for them to hear themselves read what they wrote. There are even apps that allow students to take a picture of their work, record themselves reading it, and send it to their parents. Now you've added joy to their parents' day too!

Author Studies

Using author studies can help motivate a child to read! Introducing your students to different styles of reading and illustrating can open a new excitement for them. They learn that different authors have different styles. They begin to form opinions about what they prefer to read. Your students will gain confidence in choosing books for themselves because of their knowledge of authors. Kids love learning about different authors and being able to guess who wrote a book based on what they know about the authors.

Building this foundation for literacy is the most important part of learning to read! Without this foundation, our students will sink as academic rigor increases and academic skills get more challenging. A foundation of literacy is the base for holding high standards in reading, writing, and learning in the content areas. Building strong literacy skills will provide our students with best tools for finding success!

Reflect & Consider

1. Which strategy do you plan to implement in your classroom?

   _____

   _____

   _____

2. What are your most effective tools for building foundational literacy skills?

   _____

   _____

   _____

3. What is something new you learned from this chapter?

   _____

   _____

   _____

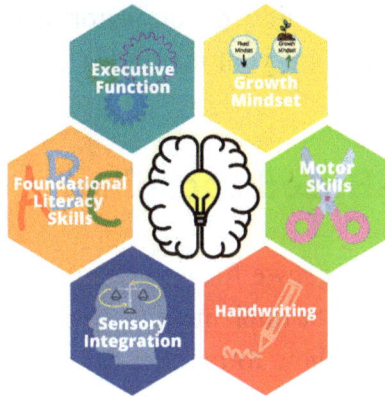

Chapter 9

Play-Based Learning

For goodness sake, let the kids play! We all love to play. Even as grown-ups, we want play time—at least I do! And I don't think I stand alone here. When you think back through the years of your own schooling, what comes to mind? Recess? Projects? Contests? Some of my favorite memories include puppet shows, playing math games on Fridays in 4th grade, learning to square dance in 5th grade, my 6th grade teacher teaching us how to play chess, my 7th grade Leaf Project, and a mock trial in high school. If you notice, none of these memories are worksheets or lectures. However, each and every one of these memories had a sense of play, whether it was make-believe, dance, or a sense of winning and losing. Play is the common denominator in each of my favorite memories. I am sure it is for your memories, too! Play makes learning memorable.

What is Play-Based Learning?

In the previous chapters, we focused on six areas of development and practical strategies for implementing them in the classroom. In this chapter, we'll learn how to make it fun. Play-based learning is learning through play! Okay, that's simple, right? Yes, it really is that simple. One of my favorite resources for my research in this topic was a book called *The Power of Play* written by David Elkind, Ph.D. Elkind states that "Love, work, and play are three inborn drives that power human thought and action." He later describes the different models for early childhood education. He believes that when we combine play, love, and work, children have the best chance of learning within their individual circumstances.

If you search the web for play-based learning, you will be flooded with great information that has been collected by researchers on how important play is to brain development and learning. One of my favorite articles, "How Play is Making a Comeback in Kindergarten," explains how The Pathfinder School in Washington state has implemented a play-based kindergarten. Like Pathfinder, many other schools in the United States have adopted this philosophy for kindergarten, some even continuing on into the older elementary grades.

Free Play

Free play is when your students get to choose what they are playing and who they are playing with. This is when children are free to use their imagination. They are able to have their own agenda for their play. For example, children may take their coats off and tie them around their neck to pretend to be a superhero or use a stick to pretend to sword fight. During free play, students can be creative, inventive, and they can even role play what they've learned in the past.

While a child is playing, they often can solve problems as they occur. Students learn to share, communicate, collaborate, make good choices, and even learn to work through bad choices. Free play is a tool that develops the whole child, and it is an important part of growing up to be an effective and efficient learner. Free play can be provided to students as part of your classroom time. However, most students only experience free play when they are at recess. In fact, many elementary schools have taken recess away from upper elementary grades. Free play is something that we should have scheduled into every school day for every elementary age student!

Guided Play

Guided play is planned and organized by the teacher for a purpose. With guided play, the teacher is in charge of setting up the space and materials with a goal for learning in mind. In most elementary classrooms this happens during learning centers or stations where there are toys and tools which engage students and foster specific learning goals. Many teachers that I've worked with have also chosen to schedule Fridays as a day for hands-on learning and play-like activities.

Together, free play and guided play will help students spark an interest, initiate a task, stay engaged, interact and communicate with their peers, and make connections. This, my friends, is when learning is at its best. Play-based learning makes learning memorable for your students.

We are on the brink of a turn in early childhood dducation. Many schools in other countries have always taught students in early childhood education through play-based methods. There are a handful of schools here in the United States that have taken on the challenge to implement more *play* in order to *learn*. Some are even dedicating their primary buildings or kindergarten centers to developing the whole child through play-based learning. Those who invented early childhood education (e.g., Maria Montessori and Friedrich Froebel) used methods such as open-ended craft projects, trial and error, insight, making observations, hypothesis testing, hands-on activities, self-directed learning, play, and curiosity. Methods such as these are still used in schools today. However, they have been placed on the back burner and only accessed when there is extra time. So, we have to ask ourselves, "Is play an extra or an essential?" Can we treat it as an essential in a time when academic rigor has taken over?

Why is Play-Based Learning important?

I think we can all agree from our own experiences in school that play is fun. I know that we can also agree that we are more likely to remember what we learned if we had fun while learning it. Play allows us to apply what we know and to take risks that will teach us more! Let's dig a bit deeper into why play is really so important.

There are three reasons play is important for learning:
1. Makes learning fun and memorable.
2. Promotes use of creativity, imagination, and problem solving.
3. Improves cognitive development in concentration, attention, perception, and memory.

Basically, kids learn through memorable, imaginative, and fun experiences. Let's face it, play is memorable and fun. So here is the big aha! moment: Play = Learning!

Okay, so maybe not a big aha moment. Maybe you read this and are thinking, "Duh! Way to state the obvious!" So why do we hear teachers say there is no time for play? Why do many have the belief that play is an extra? Why is developing a full paragraph by the end of kindergarten more important than developing memorable and fun experiences that develop cognitive skills? Why are many school principals taking away recess time? Why?

As you can tell, I am passionate about the idea that we have to make play an essential part of the classroom! And let me say it again. Play is an essential, not an extra!

There are two things that we all have in common:
1. Everyone loves to play!
2. Everyone needs to learn!

In my opinion, this is a no-brainer! We need to learn. We love to play. We learn best through memorable, fun, playful experiences. So how can we use this to our advantage?

We can let the kids *play!*

How to Implement Play-Based Learning

We can easily implement play-based learning in our school day. In grades K-5 students should be given optimal time for play. Even adults need play time! So, we should never believe that a student is too old to play. Play time will look different for each age group. If we look at play time as "Play to Learn Time," does that make you feel better about allowing your elementary kids time for play? I would even venture to say that high school students benefit from play time.

I'm thinking of a time when I was sitting in a training session for a new robotics program that our district was going to be implementing. The instructor had all of the pieces and parts in the middle of the tables that we were sitting at. We all sat down with our coffee and notepads and reached for the robotics to look, touch, inquire, and explore the pieces we knew nothing about. You see, even as adults, it is in our nature to want to play when we see something cool!

I'd like to show you just how easy it is to intentionally plan for play in your school day. In fact, I'm sure that you already have some of these "play-based practices" in place. If not, I'm willing to bet that you have certain parts of your day that could easily transform into play-based learning.

Implementing Free Play

Free play is an easy place to begin. Elementary-age kids need at least three hours of free play time throughout their day. We can assume that they get at least one hour of play at home after school. This means we need to consider offering our elementary students at least two hours (120 minutes) of free play within our school day.

Think about your school day. What do your students do when they first walk in the door? What do they do at the very end of the day? How many times do they go to recess? How long are they at recess? We can start by answering all of these questions. I asked several teachers to do just that. Here is what they reported back about the free play their students get on a daily basis.

Minutes of Free Play Per Day

Kindergarten = 100 min.	3rd Grade = 70 min.	5th Grade = 40 min.
AM Recess (20 min.)	AM Recess (20 min.)	Lunch Recess (20 min.)
Lunch Recess (20 min.)	Lunch Recess (20 min.)	PM Recess (20 min.)
PM Recess (20 min.)	PM Recess (20 min.)	
Stations (40 min.)	Pack up free time (10 min.)	

You can see from the chart that it seems that the K-3 students are most likely given a sufficient amount of free play time. However, as the students move up in grade levels, they are getting less and less free play time. Now, I know that play looks different for a 5th grader than it does for a kindergartener. However, I know that developmentally, 5th graders still need time to create, imagine, communicate, and problem solve freely. If your class isn't getting between 1-2 hours (60-120 minutes) of free play each day, you might want to be more intentional about scheduling free play into your day.

These are the easiest ways to implement free play into your school day, no matter the age or grade level:

Arrival Time

You can have pre-planned materials that you put out for your students to explore, or you can teach them a process for coming in and getting ready for their day and going to a Free Choice Play Activity. This can include jigsaw puzzles, board games, card games, playdough, blocks, LEGOS, dolls, stuffed animals. Believe it or not, if you put a bunch of materials in the middle of a table, students of any age will want to play with them.

Recess

Everyone needs a break and recess is the best kind of break. This is where so many developmental things happen that we cannot see right away. Motor skills are developed on the playground. Explorations are conducted. Imaginations and creativity are used and developed, along with building relationships, collaboration, and communication. Recess is vital! Do you need to add a recess? Get creative and get them playing!

Dismissal Time

We all have that waiting time at the end of the day. Why not let them play? Some easy dismissal time play may include tic-tac-toe, card games, LEGOS, puzzles, and so on.

Pre/Post Lesson

This is my favorite way to sneak in more play. Before or after teaching a concept, let your students play with the materials or concepts that were learned! Let them explore materials before the lesson to create a curiosity and/or understanding. Play around with the concept that was learned! If you teach them about short vowels, let them play around with short vowels. If you teach them shapes, let them play and create with shapes. If you teach a lesson on fractions, let them play or create something with fractions. Let them play!

Play to Learn

The ideas we just discussed can easily be done in *any* grade level! These are easy ways to let your kids have some free play time that will promote excitement, learning, and development. In the younger elementary grades, there is a greater need for play-based learning. The idea that we can play to learn is being considered and put into action in many schools in the United States. Teachers are being intentional about teaching the curriculum through play, by creating a time of the day called "Play to Learn!" Doesn't that sound fun?

Play to Learn is simply a short period of time throughout the day where kids get to be kids and play! The students are taught that we learn from every interaction we encounter throughout our day, and the same is true for play. Play to Learn should consist of free play, reflections, and share time. While the students are at Play to Learn, they have the freedom to play freely but are also expected to reflect on something they learned. Last, they share with the class what they learned. You may consider setting limits (e.g., a four-person limit) at each area. After the students have time to play, take 10 minutes to let the students report what they learned during their Play to Learn Time. They may say, "I was in the kitchen area with my friend, and I learned that Joey does not like pancakes, which are my favorite!" or "I learned that you cannot build a tall tower if your small blocks are on the bottom and big blocks are on the top." They may just share what they did or created. There you have it! Learning and development happening all on its own!

Play to Learn is best executed when your classroom is designed with specific play areas that may include: play kitchen area, block area, dress up area, fabric play, playdough, art area, light table, puppet show area, LEGO area, musical instruments, different textures, stamps and markers, drawing table, cars and trucks, simple machines, board games, and so on. For upper elementary grades, you could use board games, puzzles, decks of cards, and chess. The amount of time given for Play to Learn will vary based on your grade level and your schedule. In the younger grades, try to get at least 30 minutes of free play scheduled each day!

Implementing Guided Play

Child-led Guided Play

Child-led guided play occurs when the students are given materials to explore freely, and while they are immersed in play, the teacher stops by to ask questions, instruct, and prompt them to come to the goal of the play activity.

Let's say you give a group of students a basket full of blocks to play with. You give them some time to explore and then walk over to the group and ask them to work together to build one house with their blocks. Then you notice that each student in the group begins to build their own house. You might interject by saying, "I really like how you all are building a house! Now, can you all work together to build one house?" You could also say something like, "Bobby has a nice foundation or floor built. Could you all add walls to his foundation? What else will the house need other than a floor and walls?" These promptings will guide them to continue with their playing in order to complete the goal at hand. You then walk away and allow them to collaborate. Check in again later to see how they are doing.

You may get playdough out in your writing center. I actually did this in my third-grade class—yes, 3rd graders still love playdough! Tell the kids to create anything they want. Walk around and see what they are creating. Let's say you want to practice using adjectives to make their writing better. Ask them to use their creation to write a descriptive paragraph. They could even combine their playdough creations to write a collaborative story! Now we have 3rd graders who are having fun and developing academic skills, all while getting creative! Sounds to me like guided play at work!

While the students are playing at the kitchen area, you stop over to see how they are doing. You have been working on CVC (consonant, vowel, consonant) words. You ask the students in the group to each find an item that they think may be a CVC word and you have them spell it for you. You have also been working on adding in math. You grab a couple of play food items and put them on a plate. You say, "I have two donuts and three cookies on my plate. How many is that altogether? Is that enough for our group to share equally? Do we have enough? Are there some left over? What do I have more of?"

Posing questions is one way to guide them to learn or practice the specific skills that you are working on. You do not have to have them write anything down. You can just play, ask questions, have conversations, and enjoy the time together! Teachers can use this time to observe student behaviors, assess student understanding of skills, and also to work on independent skills with individual students.

Teacher-led Guided Play

I'm willing to bet you already have guided play in your classroom. In fact, if you have centers in your classroom, you probably have guided play! However, there are times when centers are not considered play at all. If you have centers set up in your room that consist of sitting in a specific spot, for a specific amount of time, doing a worksheet, this is not play. Rather, it is a way of organizing groups to complete tasks. There are many different times and ways to incorporate guided play.

Chapter 9: Play-Based Learning

The following are different ways I've observed teachers using guided play in their own classrooms:

Whole Group Lessons

You provide materials and time for the students to explore before, during and after a whole group lesson. Let's say you teach 2nd grade and you are going to introduce the terms "base, face, vertices, and edges" during your math lesson. You might put a set of building blocks in the middle of the learning space. Allow your students to play with these blocks for a few minutes before you begin. Get the students' attention and ask them what they noticed about the blocks. Give them time to share. You can review the names of the 3D Shapes, sort them by shape, and then introduce the vocabulary words. After you teach the lesson, give them more time to play, but this time give them instructions. You might have them count the bases and sort them. You might have them work to create labeling cards that list the number of bases, faces, vertices, and edges. You might have them trace the bases of each 3D shape. Then after they have completed the task, you give them a few more minutes of free play, clean up, and move on!

Fine Motor Bins

I explained this in the chapter about Fine Motor Skills. Fine motor bins are a type of guided play that can be used for pretty much any learning objective! These are bins or drawers that have specific materials to explore that will build and develop fine motor skills. This is something that would be used in the early elementary grades. However, they are fun, hands-on activities that feel like play. They include sewing, playdough, nuts and bolts, toothpicks, Q-tips, paint, clay, pegboards, Lite-Brites, and so on. Sounds like play, right?

If your class is working on adding and subtracting, you may place small little objects or counters in a bin with a +/- dice, plastic tweezers, and two dixie cups. The idea is for a student to play with a partner to see who can fill their cup first with the small items by rolling the die to see how many pieces they add or subtract to their cup using the tweezers. Purposeful, guided play in action!

Centers

There are a million different ways to organize and plan learning centers. You take the learning goals, find a game or exploration, and let the kids play and learn. This can be done in any content area. Some things to consider when planning play-based centers:

- *Engaging materials*—The students should be excited to dive in, grab the materials and get to work learning. Think of tools or items that kids just love to get their hands on! Those are tools you use in your centers.
- *Play games*—Can they play to win? This is a fun motivator for learning, but games don't have to have a winner. Some kids cannot handle the competition. Just play games that practice and review concepts.
- *Construct*—Provide an opportunity for students to construct or make something.
- *Move*—Kids need to move. Let them move around, lay on the rug, change locations, and so on.

Experiments

Use experiments as guided play. Allow your kids to explore and conduct experiments. This doesn't just mean in science class. You can experiment with anything! Get creative! Write about it, draw about it, and perform the experiment.

STEM/STEAM Activities

Provide opportunities for your students to become scientists! Use science, technology, engineering, arts, and math to teach and enrich learning skills. Often, I hear teachers say that they don't have enough time to do this type of "extra" learning. And yet, there are so many ways that you can pull STEM/STEAM into your curriculum! Here are five simple ways:

- *Robotics and Language Arts* — If you have robots to build at your school you can use them to travel to letters and sounds, show events of a story, or code it to do a task.
- *Friday STEM/STEAM DAY* — My team of teachers have used Fridays as a day dedicated to STEAM. This feels like a full day of play, and it feels that way because it is! We set up different stations and the kids go to the different stations throughout the day. Don't worry! They are still reading, writing, and thinking. It feels like play, but it's really learning in action.
- *Math Centers* — This is probably the easiest way to implement guided play. Start with the weekly goals, plan games, provide materials, and watch the learning happen!
- *Art Center* — If you don't have an easel, get one. Or just provide fun art materials and see what they can create!
- *Exploration Station* — This is where you set up a station in the classroom where students can visit when they have completed a task. I've used Cubelets, LEGOs, LEGO WeDo, and random pieces and parts. This station needs to be something the kids want to do. They can visit this station at any time during the week when they've completed their work.

Intentional Planning for Play

Being intentional about planning for play in your classroom doesn't mean that you have to fill out an additional lesson plan or change how you organize your lesson plans. It simply means that when you sit down to map out your week, in addition to considering learning goals you should also consider the amount of play your students will be getting, both free and guided play. Consider these questions when planning for play:

- What are the weekly learning goals?
- How can play promote learning of this goal?
- What is one whole group lesson that you plan to incorporate play into (both free play and guided play)?
- What skills do you plan to observe or assess while your students play?

When you write your lesson plans, it's a good idea to mark the areas of play and your intentions for it. For example, a fellow teacher of mine will put a green asterisk next to items on her lesson plans that are intentional play. I've also known teachers who change the font color of an item in their lesson plans to show that a skill is being assessed. You could do this to show skills to observe or assess during Learn to Play. This will provide a quick visual of how much play you have integrated into your daily objectives in your lesson plans.

Many school districts in the United States are making the change to play-based learning. Will your district be one of them? Is it a shift in the paradigm that you are willing to make? Many districts are reporting that play-based learning is leading to more collaborative learners with better achievement scores. If we start small and work toward a play-based learning environment in grades K-3, then shift to project-based instruction from 4th grade up, we will be tackling learning standards in a developmentally appropriate way. This will provide a better opportunity for students to achieve academic standards as well become healthy well-rounded individuals.

Who likes to play? EVERYONE!
Who needs to learn? EVERYONE!
Play = Learning

Reflect & Consider

1. How much free play time do your students get? Is it more or less than the average shown in the chart in this chapter?

   _____

   _____

   _____

2. Do you use play for learning? How can you be more intentional about implementing play for learning?

   _____

   _____

   _____

3. What is one thing that you read about in this chapter that you could implement right now in your classroom?

   _____

   _____

   _____

PART THREE

Big Moves: Developmentally Appropriate Pedagogy

I n this section, we will focus on specific things you can do daily (or weekly) to support your students' development. These are what I call "Big Moves." They will take a little more effort on your part. You may have to have an open mind and let your love for teaching shine! You may need to shift your own philosophy of teaching in order to orient your class toward students' developmental success.

Part Three will make you think about your approach to teaching students the standards that are given to you. Yes, we are all required to teach the standards. Yes, most school districts have bought textbooks to use for your instruction. These textbooks are research-based and usually have a lot to offer, as far as differentiating for variability and making learning fun and creative. However, some districts' textbooks are from when I was in school (and you can probably figure out how long ago that was), while other districts have stopped purchasing textbooks because of budget costs. And let's face it, teachers are great at creating their own teaching tools! I mean, look at what has become of sites like Teachers Pay Teachers! Let's face it, teachers. When teachers see a need, they create a solution! I don't know a teacher out there who hasn't either created their own materials or bought teacher-made materials.

You will want to consider your choices for your teaching approach—the *big moves* we make to reach our students and help them develop and grow. This is pedagogy, defined as "the art, science, or profession of teaching." There are so many things that go into the profession of teaching, but pedagogy is essentially your teaching method. There are many moving parts to pedagogy that include teaching styles, feedback, and assessment. The commitment to how you teach is a big deal. It's a move from teaching standards to teaching kids. It's the "how" you teach rather than the "what" you teach.

I would like to guide you through some developmentally appropriate teaching pedagogies that will help you create an environment where kids learn organically from their natural curiosity, while you teach the standards that are required. Let's teach the standards, but more importantly, let's do it in a way that also teaches the kids.

CHAPTER 10

Three Pedagogies for Teaching and Learning: PrBL, PBL, IBL

About six years into my career, I was presented with the opportunity to pilot a new type of classroom in our elementary school. They were calling it "Project-Based Learning." A colleague and I did a little research, and then observed a 4th grade class that was already operating this way, and we were sold. We absolutely loved what we saw. Kids were working in teams solving problems, doing research, collaborating, and creating. The teachers were working with small groups of students on individual learning goals, test-taking strategies, presenting new instruction, and remediating. We were in awe of what we saw and could not wait to dive in and do it in our own 3rd grade class.

We started out with our grade level (3rd grade) state standards. We worked through the content areas and created research projects for each theme in our social studies and science state standards. As for reading and math, we decided to take the approach of pre-testing, instruction, post-testing, peer tutoring, remediation, and re-assessing for mastery. We integrated our math and reading standards as best we could into our themed research projects. However, we were responsible for continuing to follow the curriculum map created and used by the others in our grade level team.

Our classroom was made up of 46 students. Now, I know that sounds like a lot, but there were two of us. I cannot emphasize enough the value of having two teachers in one classroom. This gave us a tremendous amount of time for small group instruction and remediation. While our students were in groups working on projects, the teachers were either facilitating, instructing small groups, or working with students who needed remediation. This style of learning kept our students engaged and excited about learning. They took the research projects to a higher level than we ever expected. There were times that the students branched off on their own to conduct independent research, other times when they were assigned different roles, and other times when they oversaw creating the project and executing it. This style of teaching and learning provided the teachers with the opportunity to ensure that no child slipped through the cracks. Parents, students, and, of course, the teachers loved this style of teaching. The requests to be in this classroom were overwhelming.

There are many different methods, processes, and strategies that engage learning. Problem-Based Learning (PrBL), Project -Based Learning (PBL), and Inquiry-Based Learning (IBL) are three that have many similarities, though they are not the same. These different processes for learning can be used in different scenarios and are more purposeful and fitting for different stages of learning.

Let's explore the similarities and differences:

Comparison of Three Teaching Pedagogies

Problem-Based Learning (PrBL)	- Students are called to solve real world problems. - Students come up with viable solutions to define problems. - The process = investigate, test, discover, repeat. - Students are investigators.
Project-Based Learning (PBL)	- Long-term program that works on real world problems. - Students work to produce a tangible product. - Students investigate, collaborate, and create products.
Inquiry-Based Learning (IBL)	- Starts with a question that engages students to wonder and wonder more. - Students' responses lead to further questioning. - The process leads to deeper understanding. - Students are investigators.

These creative and engaging ways of learning will benefit the whole child. The list of benefits to teaching through PrBL, PBL, and IBL are quite lengthy. So, let me just give you a quick snapshot of some of the benefits from learning in these ways:

- Empowers students to learn more and make a difference.
- Allows students to use content and skills that can be applied to real life situations.
- Creates critical thinkers and problem solvers.
- Helps students' desire to continue the learning journey.
- Increases students' ability to research and use scanning and skimming to do so.
- Students gain fluency and accuracy in seeking information and sharing their findings.
- Students become collaborators and good communicators.
- Students become self-aware of their learning and success.
- Students are happy and motivated to learn.
- Builds students' confidence.
- Empowers students to love learning!

Each of these pedagogies can be used in any grade level, and it is acceptable to use all methods when it fits the situation. Read an example of how each method can be used in a primary classroom.

Problem-Based Learning (PrBL)

In Early Childhood you can take real problems that are meaningful to your students and use them for engaged learning. For example, I mentioned earlier the story of the classroom hamster who went missing in Mrs. C's class! They had a big problem. This was *real*! It was a huge distraction for the class. Rather than tell the students that they needed to focus and move on to their learning for the day, she changed directions. She brainstormed with her students to find ways to find a missing hamster. The class decided to build a ramp going up to his cage, with treats to lure him in. They made posters advertising the missing hamster. They also set up a couple hamster traps. While trying to solve this problem, the kids were able to work collaboratively and creatively to solve the problem. It required them to do some research, practice writing skills, reading skills, and even a little science and math.

Project-Based Learning (PBL)

Young Learners can work on long-term projects! They will need some guidance and assistance of course, but they definitely are capable. For example, Poetry Cafe is one project that I have seen used in grades K-3. The students learn all about poetry and the project is to plan a Poetry Cafe. In order to do this, they need to learn what a Poetry Cafe is, plan the day and time, plan the presentations, make invitations, organize and plan the space, and plan the presentations and how they will be executed. In addition, they need to practice their presentations and be ready to perform for the audience! This involved planning, research, writing, organizing, a variety of literacy skills, and so much more!

Inquiry-Based Learning (IBL)

Young Learners ask questions because they are curious and want to learn about various things. You can guide them toward their learning standards, but it's their own curiosities that truly guide the unit. For example, the teacher reads a story to the class about day and night. The students are excited about nighttime. They are intrigued by the sky at night and want to share all their stories, experiences, and questions. One student shares that he saw a shooting star over the weekend. The rest of the class gets excited about it and wants to talk more. In this situation the teacher starts to write down all the things that her class "wonders" about the night sky. After they have generated a list of their questions, they start to do some discovering. The teacher guides them through the process of answering their questions by providing experiences, books, and other materials to do so. They continue this process until they come to a conclusion of learning. They finish the process by creating something to show what they have learned and share it with others. A unit like this starts with one theme (Day and Night) and can go in many directions depending on the curiosity of the class. I've used this unit several times and each group took it in a different direction. The bottom line is that they met the standards, they were in control of their learning, they gained confidence, and they were researchers, discoverers, collaborators, and creators. The learning goals were met in a fun and memorable way.

PrBL and PBL are easily implemented in Pre-K through 3rd grade as specific situations occur. However, I believe that inquiry-based learning (IBL) is the most natural way for young learners to gain the knowledge and learn from the experiences we plan for them. Young learners are the most curious learners. They have little experience and knowledge and are craving to know about everything. They are sponges. We simply use their questions to guide us through the year of learning. You could orchestrate your entire year of learning using inquiry-based learning. Yes, my friends, your entire year! The kids will love it and so will you!

I know, I know, you are thinking "but what about the state standards?" "Show me how to teach CVC words or word families through inquiry." "What about adding, perimeter and area, nouns and verbs?" You may initially think that all the state standards that you are responsible for cannot be taught through problems, projects, and inquiry—and you are right. There is definitely a need for traditional instruction through mini-lessons, whole group, small group, and centers. But all of the academic standards can be developed through these different pedagogies. I will walk you through the process of inquiry-based learning in the next chapter because it seems to be the most natural way for primary age children to learn.

CHAPTER 11

Inquiry-Based Learning for Elementary Classrooms

Kids are so curious! It seems that they are always asking questions. Have you ever considered letting their questions drive your instruction? In fact, there have been several times in my career when I set out to teach something in a certain way and ended up teaching something completely different because of my students' curiosities. I have a confession to make—when this happened, although it felt fun and fulfilling, I also felt a tremendous amount of guilt, as if I had broken a rule. I didn't follow the manual. I strayed from the original plan. I actually felt guilty that the "learning packet" that my team spent hours creating never got opened. (Oops! Handout 1.4 didn't get completed because my kids had so many questions that they led me astray!) Okay, people, there is something wrong with this! I know that I am not the only teacher who has felt this way before.

We have been trained to dissect the state standards, analyzing each and every word so that we can do it the best. We have agreed to complete the same handout as each teacher on our team. But why? Why are we doing this when we could be having fun and getting the same results or better?

Kids are curious. Kids want to know more. They have a natural curiosity that will teach them so much more than any handout or learning packet that we have to offer them. Students enjoy discovering new things and exploring their natural curiosities. So why not take a step back and ask them what they want to know? Ask them how they think we could discover answers to their questions. Why not ask our students to drive our teaching? We can! We can do just that while we have fun in the process. And inquiry-based learning is the way to do just that!

What is Inquiry-Based Learning?

Inquiry-based learning (IBL) is a student-centered process for learning that has been around since the 1960's. It is a way of learning through curiosity, asking questions, investigating, exploring, and generating even more questions. The students become active participants in investigating and taking responsibility for gaining knowledge on the topic at hand. This way of learning allows students to fully comprehend the meaning of what is being learned. Rather than memorizing what is taught to them, the students are able to share their questions and dig deep to get answers. This will lead to a deeper understanding of the content. IBL is not a teaching technique; it is a process or pedagogy for learning. Allow me to walk you through the process that I discovered worked in my own elementary classroom.

How to Use IBL in Your Classroom

Start With a Broad Idea

Your broad idea can come from your students' interests and curiosities, or you can orchestrate a way to spark their interest in a topic of your choice. Because public school teachers are obligated to teach certain topics in each grade level, your social studies and science standards or seasonal and monthly themes are a great place to start. Rather than telling your class what they are about to learn, you present them with something that will trigger questions and natural curiosity in your students. You can create an inquiry unit of study that aligns with your standards, while allowing the students to take the lead. The more you teach in this way, the better you will feel about not spoon-feeding your students the state standards.

For example: If you are responsible for teaching the four seasons and differentiating between them, you might use "seasons" as your broad theme and allow your students to take it in whatever directions they are interested. They may be interested in what to wear during each season. They could choose weather. They may be interested in what the trees or plants and animals do in the different seasons. Or maybe they are super curious about why we have seasons. Let them create the path they want to follow in order to study the broad theme mapped out in your state standards.

Spark Students' Interest

Plan for a way to spark interest in order to get students to start thinking about your theme. Ask them what they wonder about the topic you have in mind. Make it fun! Go for a walk outside or while you are at recess, initiate conversation that may get them talking more or thinking more about your broad topic. You can set up experiences for them to explore during play. You want to find out what your students know about the broad theme and what sparks their interest, keeping in mind your goal for learning. You can see how to dig deeper by using a KWL chart, Wonder Web, or a simple plain piece of paper.

KWL Chart

This is a great way to spark your kids' curiosity. Kids love to share what they already know about something. This typically engages other students to think about the topic and share their knowledge and curiosities. As the teacher, you basically scribe what the students are saying about the topic using a KWL chart or just making a list:

What do I Know?	What do I want to know?	What did I learn?
- No school in the summer - Stays light outside later - Gets dark earlier - Some are cold and some are hot - You need air conditioner in the summer - I go swimming in summer. - Leaves fall in the fall - Pretty flowers in spring	- Why is it warm in summer? - How many seasons are there? - Why do the leaves change colors? - Why does it stay light so late in the summer? - Why do some trees change and some stay the same?	

Wonder Web

This is my favorite way to begin an inquiry unit. You write the theme in the middle of the web. Ask the students what they want to know or what they "wonder" about your theme. This is really fun! You write down all of their curiosities around the center of the "I Wonder..." bubble. In this example you see that our class wrote the question, "What can we build with blocks?" in the center of our web. First, we explored with our set of classroom blocks. The kids were able to experiment with building different types of structures.

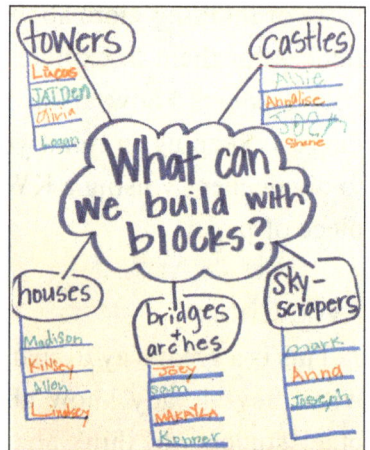

- 196 -

They were really interested in castles and bridges. This led to investigating architecture through literacy. We studied photos of different types of structures, read books about engineering and architecture, and watched BrainPOP lessons about different architectural structures.

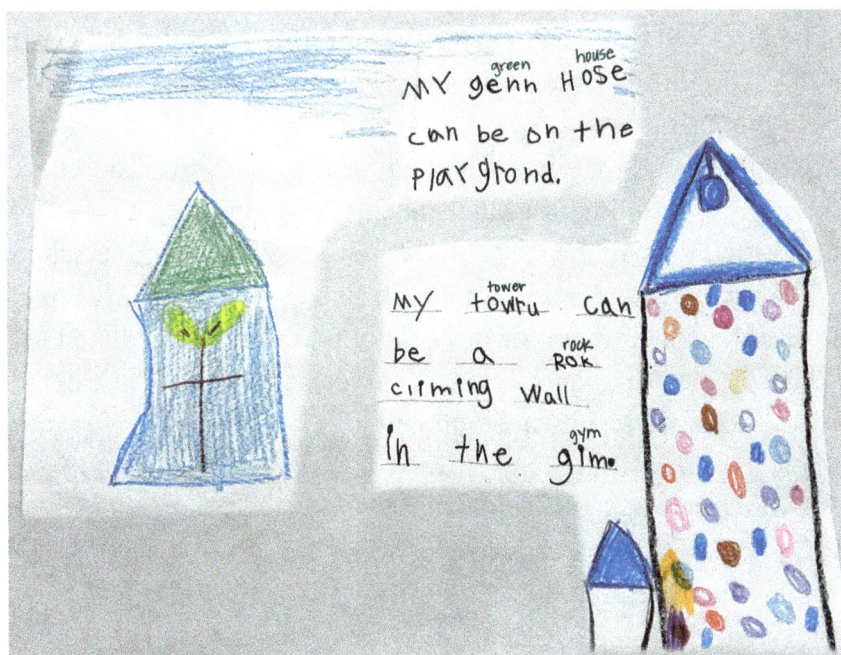

After doing some research of different types of structures, the kids brainstormed six different types of structures that they thought were interesting and they were able to build with blocks. Each student signed up to become an expert on one type of structure: homes, castles, factories, towers, skyscrapers, arches, and bridges. You can see that they actually came up and signed their name next to the topic that was of interest to them. The students decided that they wanted to make their own structures out of recycled materials. This added time to the project, but the kids were having a blast and came up with the most amazing ideas! They brought in all types of cardboard boxes. We tried building with them to see which were sturdy and which were not. We repaired some boxes and painted them. The kids decided to sort them by shape and design them so that each shape had a different color of design on them. This was fun and messy! Once the student-made blocks were done, we started building. The students were able to build their structure, take a picture of it, and create a blueprint for their structure. Our 2nd grade friends came to help us label the 3D Shapes. This was quite the geometry lesson for both grade levels. Students took pride in sketching and labeling these blueprints.

We presented our blueprints and structures to local architects. This was so meaningful to the students. Each group gave a reason their structure should be used in the new renovations of our school.

The architects talked about which structures would most likely fit into the construction of our school that they had planned.

This project was planned to last two weeks. However, the kids took it very seriously and it ended up going into a third week. The key is that the kids were driving the unit. It all started with geometry standards, an obsession with architecture and our school being renovated, and the excitement of a class of kindergarteners. They learned so much during this lesson!

Plain Piece of Paper

Another great way to spark their interest when starting an inquiry unit is to simply pass out a plain half-sheet of paper to each student. First, tell them your topic or broad idea and ask them to draw or write anything that they know about the topic. The next step is to start to ask questions about their drawings. The key here is to do more listening than talking. Allow your students to lead this discussion about what they think is true and new questions they may be wondering about in regard to the pictures made by the class. You start to see similarities in what they know and what they do not know.

In this stage you can start to organize categories or subtopics that are interesting to your class. You can map it out on chart paper to use as a visual. You can sort all of your students' questions into the categories. This will show you all what you need to investigate and discover.

Investigate and Discover

Authoritative Sources

You will provide resources that your students can use to find out more about their questions. You can use books, photos, videos, lessons that you teach and lessons from the web. You can also call in an expert or take a trip to investigate or discover. In this step the students are investigators! They often find answers that lead to more questions. You continue this process until you come to your conclusion about your topic.

The investigation phase of IBL is the perfect time to pull in the other learning standards to strengthen and develop. During their investigations you can work on phonics skills, reading, writing, and math! Some great ways to do this are listed below.

Centers

Learning Centers are a great part of the day to integrate your students investigations and research with other content areas like reading, writing, spelling, and even math. Reading and writing can always be integrated into IBL projects. Simply take your regular planned centers and use your IBL unit as the subject to focus on. They can read to investigate, draw to document their findings, and write all about what they are learning. Some ideas for how to use centers during the investigation phase of IBL are listed below:

- Study photos of the inquiry topics. They can make observations and write about what they discover.

- Do partner reading on books about the topic.
- Write about what they have discovered.
- Create a model, painting, or diagram to show their learning or ideas.
- Read both fiction and nonfiction books that fit your topic and have discussions about different genres.
- Conduct experiments or investigations for discovery.
- Search for word families or other phonics skills that have been taught.
- Build structures and creations.
- Measure and calculate.

Guided Reading

Use this time to meet with partners or groups that are working on an investigation. Read leveled books with your group that are about the topic and work on specific parts of your IBL process with your small group. Teach new phonics skills to your group while tying it in with your topic. If you choose to make expert groups in each category, you can use this time to meet with the small expert groups to go over their findings.

Show What You Know!

As a group, decide how you want to show what you know. Part of IBL is sharing your knowledge with others. You can use different graphic organizers and maps to show what the students have discovered. Then they take what they learned and create something to show it. Some great ideas I've seen students come up with include:

- *Classroom Museums*—Turn your classroom into a museum and invite others to visit.
- *Parades*—Parade through your school showing what you've learned.

- *Plays*—Conduct a play and invite guests.
- *Presentations*—Invite parents, staff, or other classrooms to see you present your discoveries.
- *Google Slides*—Present google slides to their peers or to other classrooms of students.
- *Posters and Bulletin Boards*—Create a bulletin board that displays your questions and discoveries in your hallway for all to see.
- *Classroom*—Turn your classroom into a habitat for others to visit and explore.

Inquiry-based learning is so much fun for both teachers and students. Students are engaged because they are the driving force for discovering. Many teachers are nervous about letting students take the lead. However, you quickly learn that you can still conquer every learning goal while letting students' inquiries lead the unit.

Once I started to experiment with this method, I couldn't go back to the "old" way. I found that you can meet all of your standards, with the bonus of developing the whole child. Inquiry-based learning provides an opportunity for the students to develop executive function skills and 21st Century skills, and also provides opportunities for you to promote a growth mindset through the inquiry process. You will observe your students' self-confidence and developmental skills mature and strengthen along the way. When all of this happens, you will witness greatness in both learning and teaching!

Reflect & Consider

1. What broad idea could you turn into an IBL unit?

_____

_____

_____

2. What will be the driving question for this IBL unit?

_____

_____

_____

3. What resources do you have that your students could use for the investigate and discover part of your unit?

_____

_____

_____

CONCLUSION

Slow the Heck Down!

C an you hear the passion in my voice? I hope you can see just how important this is. Slow down. Let your students develop. Let them play and have fun—that is how kids learn. Teach them strategies for gaining a positive perspective. Help them to believe that they can do hard things!

Don't forget about my former student, Brian. I can't help but wonder if he had been given the tools to train his brain to handle the hard stuff, if he was striving for his own personal best rather than perfection, would his first year of college have been different?

It all started with that question. After finding out that Brian considered self-harm, along with experiencing my own son's anxiety levels about school, and then realizing how much the standards have changed in the nearly 20 years that I have been teaching, I started to ask more questions. What can we do to minimize students' stress? Why do they feel like they have to handle it all? Where have we gone wrong? How can we try to fix it? When do students start to feel this pressure? What would happen if Early Childhood Teachers slowed down to focus on developmental skills?

And there it was, the driving question for this book: How can I create an awareness in education and support teachers in understanding the importance of slowing down and focusing on developmental growth to prepare students for the hustle beyond 3rd grade?

I considered what I knew:
- I knew that students' anxiety rates (and suicide rates, by the way) are higher than ever before.
- I knew that some school districts' mentality of "race to the top" has forced teachers to replace certain learning activities with more complex academics.
- I knew that in primary education, the standards are higher than ever before, while the development of kids remains the same.
- I knew that developing the brain's frontal lobe would enable students to be better organized, focused, and in control of their inhibitions.
- I knew that teaching students about perception and mindset would make all the difference.
- I knew that you can't expect a student to write a paragraph if they don't have the muscle control and strength in their hands to do the writing.
- I knew that children are curious. They have a need to explore and discover.
- I knew that science, technology, engineering, arts, and math are necessary for 21st century.learners.
- I knew that kids need to have fun.
- I knew that teachers needed to know they are doing what is best for their students.

In response to this driving question, I knew that slowing down to focus on developmental growth would make a difference. Just as an archer slowly pulls the arrow back, taking time to focus on what is important, we can hit our targeted goals by doing the same—slowing down to focus on developing the following areas in order to make all the difference in the learning process for our students:

- Executive Function Skills
- Growth Mindset
- Motor Skills
- Handwriting
- Sensory Integration
- Foundations of Literacy
- Play-Based Learning
- Our Own Teaching Pedagogy

> *"Everyone who comes to me and hears my words
> and does them, I will show you what he is like:
> he is like a man building a house, who dug deep and
> laid the foundation on the rock. And when a flood arose,
> the stream broke against that house and could not shake
> it, because it had been well built. But the one who
> hears and does not do them is like a man who built a
> house on the ground without a foundation.
> When the stream broke against it, immediately it fell,
> and the ruin of that house was great."*
> —Luke 6:47-49

There you go—I went and quoted the Bible! It doesn't get much wiser than that, does it? And hopefully you get my point: Take the time to build that foundation, folks! Without a strong foundation, our kids might fail and the ruin could be great. In a time when education has become so fast-paced, are you ready to be the one who slows down, builds the foundation, equips your students developmentally, and makes a difference?

You can be their difference by establishing the foundation for learning, encouraging them along the way, and applauding them when they achieve.

Slow Down! Children are Learning!

About the Author

Erin Mengeu has enjoyed teaching and inspiring kids for 20 years. She has been an elementary classroom teacher in many different classroom settings, including Project-Based Learning, co-teaching experiences, and full inclusion. She earned her B.A. in Education from Mount Union College in Ohio, and an M.A. from Marygrove University in Michigan. Erin has lead collaborative teams of teachers that she taught with through the years and now teaches graduate courses for educator professional development through Dominican University of California and University of Massachusetts Global. She has spent many years researching in the area of developmental growth and brain development. She is passionate about making learning fun and engaging, and about teaching kids to gain a love for learning. Erin is also currently helping teachers learn effective strategies for developmental growth through her blog, Be Their Difference, which she started in 2019. She's a proud mama to three energetic children and although Erin is a native of Ohio, she's learning to love the beauty of her new home in Michigan.

You can learn more practical strategies about developmental growth on Erin's web site at www.betheirdifference.com. You can read her blog, access teacher resources, and learn how to be your own very best educator so that you can, indeed, on behalf of your students, BE THEIR DIFFERENCE!

Acknowledgments

It's no secret that I like to share the things that I am most passionate about. Those who know me well know that my passions in life are faith, friends and family, and education. I am so fortunate to have had the opportunity to spend time reflecting, researching, and writing about what I've learned through the years of being a teacher and wanting to make a difference in the lives of those I teach. I would like to share my gratitude in that same order: faith, family and friends, and education.

Without getting too preachy on you, my first thanks goes to God! He has orchestrated my life so beautifully, placing the right people in my life at the right times. He has shown up in every aspect of my life. Thank you, Lord, for your perfect plan!

The gift of time to accomplish this work was only possible because of my husband, Todd. His drive and dedication are the reason that I have been able to be home with our children, venture into writing and instructing graduate courses for teachers, and dedicate time to research and write this book. Todd, I will be forever thankful for your support and for this gift of time and new opportunities! Thank you to Cooper, Delaney, and Hudson, my three beautiful and energetic children for being patient all those summer mornings while I was out on the porch writing. It's not always easy to be independent when mom is in sight, but you did it! I hope that you will one day let your faith and passion drive you to your own success.

Thank you to each and every wonderful educator that I have worked with. I have learned so much from every one of you. From my first year of teaching to my 18th year of teaching, I've had the opportunity to learn from the best. Kathy Tobias, Monica Westhoven, Sarah Kohlic, Mike Coldsnow, and many other specialists that shared their strategies and knowledge with me—thank you, thank you, thank you! I only wish every teacher would have the opportunity to work so closely with the specialists in their buildings.

Acknowledgments

Thank you to every amazing teacher I've worked with and learned from. I've been placed on the best teaching teams! Lisa Seddon, you are a rock star! We did some of our best work together navigating new territory in education! Alison DeGeorge and Trish DiDonato, thank you for being my voice of reason all of the times my passion got the best of me! Kaitlyn Rushin, Tina Glymph, Jeannie Bussey, thank you for always putting what's best for students first. I've learned so much from each of you. I am truly grateful for this teacher tribe of mine! You are the best of the best!

This writing journey has been long and there were many times I almost gave up, but I have the best tribe of cheerleaders! You know who you are! Thank you so much for constantly reminding me of my strengths and listening to me vent about the obstacles. Thank you for brainstorming with me, for listening to me rant when I get on my soap box, and for loving me all of the time. My friends, my family, my tribe, I love you more than you know. Thank you for being my cheerleaders and my support system.

Thank you to Peg Daisley and Dawn Daisley for helping me make this book a reality. Peg, your editing and advice were just what I needed! Dawn, the book is beautiful, thanks to you!

A Big Thanks!

Chapter Notes

Chapter 1: Fear of Failing

Age of Opportunity: Lessons from the New Science of Adolescence. Laurence Steinberg, Ph.D. An Eamon Dolan Book / Mariner Books / Houghton Mifflin Harcourt, 2015.

"Early in Life & the Importance of Early Childhood Education." You-Tube video of October 29, 2018 TEDx presentation by Steve Zwolak, CEO of the University City Children's Center, Saint Louis, MO and founder of the LUME Institute there.

"First Grade Teachers' Knowledge of Phonological Awareness and Code Concepts: Examining Gains from an Intensive Form of Professional Development and Corresponding Teacher Attitudes." Margie B. Gillis, et al. *Reading and Writing: An Interdisciplinary Journal*, vol. 22, no. 4, p. 425-455, April 2009.

"Four Pillars of NCLB [No Child Left Behind]," U.S. Department of Education, July 2014.

LUME Institute at University City Children's Center, Saint Louis, MO. Stephen P. Zwolak, M.Ed., Chief Executive Officer.

"Most U.S. Teens See Anxiety and Depression as a Major Problem Among Their Peers." Juliana Menasce Horowitz and Nikki Graf. Pew Research, February 20, 2019.

"No Child Left Behind, An Overview." Alyson Klein. *Education Week*, April 10, 2015.

"Taking Back Kindergarten: Rethinking Rigor for Young Learners." Dr. Sarah Silverman. TeachingStrategies.com, April 2019.

Chapter 2: Who's Afraid of the Big Bad Wolf? Building a Foundation for Learning

Building a Strong Foundation for Learning. Beth Carlson. NAESP, Foundation for Child Development, 2006.

"The Case of Brain Science and Guided Play: A Developing Story." Brenna Hassinger, Das Kathy Hirsh, Roberta Pasek, and Michnick Golinkoff. National Association for the Education of Young Children, 2017.

Chapter 3: Executive Function Skills

Conversational Style: Analyzing Talk Among Friends. Deborah Tannen. Oxford University Press, 2005.

"Executive Functions." Weill Institute for Neurosciences, University of California at San Francisco.

Interrupting Chicken. David Ezra Stein. Candlewick Press, 2016. Also available as a read-aloud book on YouTube.

"Staying a Beat Ahead." Kristen Jacobson and Sarah Ward. *Attention Magazine*, August 2014. Published by CHADD (Children Children and Adults with Attention-Deficit/Hyperactivity Disorder), Lanham, MD.

Unselfie: Why Empathetic Kids Succeed in Our All-About-Me World. Michele Borba, Ed.D. Touchstone, an imprint of Simon & Schuster, 2017.

"What Is Executive Function? And How Does It Relate to Child Development?" Center on the Developing Child, Harvard University.

The Zones of Regulation. Lisa Kuypers. Think Social Publishing, 2011, and Zonesofregulation.com

Chapter 4: Growth Mindset

Growth Mindset Playbook: A Teacher's Guide to Promoting Student Success. Annie Brock and Heather Hundley. Ulysses Press, 2017.

Mindset: The New Psychology of Success. Carol S. Dweck, Ph.D. Ballantine Books, 2007.

Chapter 5: Motor Skills

"Fine Motor Activities in Elementary School Children: A Replication Study." Sierra Caramia, Amanpreet Gill, Alisha Ohl, and David Schelly. *American Journal of Occupational Therapy*, vol. 74, no. 2, April 2020.

Chapter 6: Handwriting

"5 Brain-Based Reasons to Teach Handwriting in School." J.Richard Gentry Ph.D. *Psychology Today*, 2016.

"Why Should We Teach Handwriting?" Susan Cahill Ph.D. Lewis University Experts Blog, 2018.

Chapter 7: Sensory Integration

"How Educators can use Sensory Integration Techniques in the Classroom to Improve Focus in Young Children: Perspectives from Occupational Therapists." Alicia Thompson Noddings, B.S., B.M., M.A. UMI Dissertation Publishing, 2012.

Chapter 9: Play-Based Learning

"The Case of Brain Science and Guided Play: A Developing Story." Brenna Hassinger, Das Kathy Hirsh, Roberta Pasek, and Michnick Golinkoff. National Association for the Education of Young Children, 2017.

"How play is making a comeback in kindergarten," Jackie Mader, The Hechinger Report, February 8, 2020.

The Power of Play: Learning what comes naturally. David Elkind. Da Capa Lifelong Books, A Member of the Perseus Books Group, 2007.

Chapter 10: Three Pedagogies for Teaching and Learning: PrBL, PBL, IBL

"A comparison of inquiry-based learning (IBL), problem-based learning (PBL) and project-based learning (PJBL) in science education." Ayse Oguz-Unver and Sertac Arabacioglu. *Academia Journal of Educational Research* 2(7): 120-128, July 2014.

"IBL, PBL, and PJBL, What's the Difference?" Kimberlain Education, June 24, 2018.

Chapter 11: Inquiry-Based Learning for Elementary Classrooms

Inquiry Based Learning: From Teacher-Guided to Student-Driven." YouTube video by Edutopia, 2015.

Index

Index

G

H

L

language and literacy, 24
language processing areas in the brain, 132
language skills, 155
learning centers, 180, 199
learning standards, 131, 182, 191, 199
learning to hear and understand sounds, 157
learning to read, 87, 156-157, 160, 167
learning to type, 128, 129
learning to write in cursive, 132
legible handwriting, 131
LEGOS, 123, 175, 177, 181
letter crafts, 70
letters and sounds, 155-159, 181
librarian, 105
life skills, 9
light table, 177
listening, 9, 31, 35, 41-44, 56, 59, 61-66, 70, 102, 155, 157, 163, 167, 198
Lite-Brites, 125, 179
literacy, 9, 20, 25, 72, 131, 136, 156, 158, 166-168, 190, 197
love for learning, 29, 37
low self-esteem, 46
Lucy Listener, 63, 64

M

mail deliveries, 161
make-believe, 169
making eye contact, 65-66, 102
making predictions, 161
manuscript and cursive handwriting, 130
mapping out specific skills, 158
math, 4, 7, 52, 69, 79, 96, 97, 111-112, 119, 123, 140, 169, 178-179, 181, 187, 190, 199
measure, 54, 59, 68, 200

P

Index

" A cup of coffee and this book makes me feel like I'm connecting with a teacher friend who gets it "
— *Kali LaValla, M. Ed.*

" I highly recommend the book Slow Down! Children Are Learning! for teachers K-12. Although the book is intended for elementary teachers, building the whole child is a never-ending process, requiring each phase of learning (elementary, middle and high school) to connect. If the love for learning is achieved, children will become life learners "
— *La-Shanda West, Ed. S., iPrep Academy Leader*
Miami-Dade County Public Schools

" While reading this book, I was reminded why I became an educator. It is so easy to focus on procedures, programs, and even achievement scores that we often forget to remember that we are in the student business. Erin Mengeu reminds us that time should not be constant in the learning process, and that our goal is to put the needs of each individual student first. She reminds the reader that people (students) trump programs every time, and that 'common sense' education should be our goal. "
— *Dr. Blaine Alexander, Principal, East End Middle School /*
Sheridan, Arkansas, and Leadership Coach

" This book is an easy-read and well-researched. It's a great reminder for teachers and administrators that it is hard for students to access the learning when anxieties are at the forefront of their minds. Erin's passion for teaching and for teaching the whole child shines through! "
—*Laura Wilkowski, Elementary School Principal*

" An inspiring book about getting back to the basics of teaching early childhood education. "
—*Kaitlyn Rushin M.Ed., Ohio Kindergarten Teacher*

"Erin masterfully outlines a pathway to help teachers begin to identify, internalize, and put into action approaches which encourage improvement and advancement by taking time to slow down and allow children's brains to mature, solidify executive functioning skills, instill a growth mindset, and inspire a desire to learn. Author Mengeu's book teaches teachers and leaders to intimately focus on "little moves" which set students on a successful trajectory culminating in a lifetime of positive academic outcomes."
—*Jami Fowler-White, NBCT, Author, National Keynote Speaker, Co-Founder of Digital PD 4 You, LLC*

"Erin provides the *what?*, *why?* and *how?* of the difference-making strategies that nurture students' curiosity, positive relationships and growth mindsets. She leverages cross-disciplinary expertise to reveal the developmental importance of everyday classroom skills and tasks that may be taken for granted. *Slow Down! Children Are Learning!* sparks *a-ha!* moments, affirms effective practice, and offers a wealth of practical strategies that improve outcomes for kids—and that help educators reconnect with their passion for teaching."
—*Brad Hughes, Elementary Principal, Ontario, Canada; Training & Development Specialist, Teach Better Team; Host of* The Good News, Brad News Podcast

"A convincing rationale for focusing on important aspects of child development, like executive function, during the elementary school years, this book provides an encyclopedia of activities to support those aspects. A must-have resource for teachers!"
—*Kathy Tobias, Speech-Language Pathologist*

66 A book reminding us of the crucial need to support the whole child. They are more than a score. 99

—Tina Glymph, M.A. Kindergarten Teacher

66 In one handy resource, Erin Mengeu provides an abundance of practical, engaging instructional strategies that any teacher will appreciate. If you want to enhance the learning experience for your students, look no further than *Slow Down! Children are Learning!* 99

—Joshua Little, P. Min.

66 A quick read with meaningful content that can be applied immediately in the classroom. The information doesn't feel like 'one more thing' piled onto a teacher's workload. It feels more like a sprinkling of many, simple yet important things that make sense when it comes to building foundational skills. I love the focus on building foundational skills for learning 99

—Kali LaValla, M. Ed.

66 Reading this book is like having a conversation with an experienced, trusted colleague. It confirms what your gut tells you is best for kids and includes many practical, easy to implement strategies to help improve your classroom instruction today. 99

—Katherine Metiva, M.Ed., 3rd grade teacher (33 years)

66 Written with honesty, humor, and strong pedagogy. A must-read for today's overwhelmed educator 99

— Carly Spina, Educator, Author,
Multilingual Education Specialist

Slow Down! Children Are Learning!

Effective strategies to support overall achievement by focusing on developmental growth in elementary classrooms

Copyright © 2022
Erin Mengeu

Published by Be Their Difference
www.BeTheirDifference.com

Editing: Blue Horizon Books
www.bluehorizonbooks.com

Design: Dawn Daisley
www.morninglitebookdesign.com

Publisher's Cataloging-in-Publication data:
Mengeu, Erin
Slow Down! Children Are Learning!
Effective strategies to support overall achievement by focusing on developmental growth in elementary classrooms.
ISBN: 9798985160826